CAREER CHOICES for Students of PSYCHOLOGY

by
CAREER ASSOCIATES

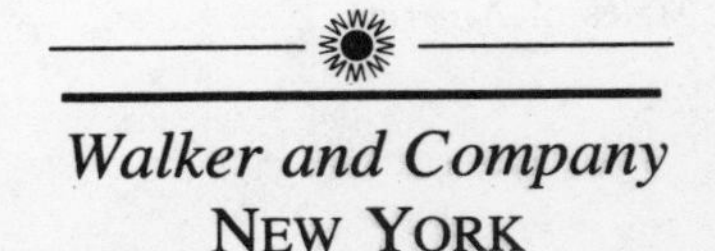

Walker and Company
NEW YORK

First published in the United States of America in 1985 by the Walker Publishing Company, Inc.

Published simultaneously in Canada by John Wiley & Sons Canada, Limited, Rexdale, Ontario.

Library of Congress Cataloging in Publication Data
Main entry under title:

Career choices for students of psychology.

Bibliography: p.
1. United States—Occupations. 2. College graduates—Employment—United States. 3. Vocational guidance—United States. I. Career Associates.
HF5382.5.U5C2556 1985 331.7′023 83-40446
ISBN 0-8027-0799-8
ISBN 0-8027-7253-6 (pbk.)

Printed in the United States of America

10 9 8 7 6 5 4 3 2 1

Titles in the Series

Career Choices for Students of:
Art
Business
Communications and Journalism
Computer Science
Economics
History
Mathematics
Political Science and Government
Psychology

Career Choices for Undergraduates Considering:
Law
An M.B.A.

Acknowledgments

We gratefully acknowledge the help of the many people who spent time talking to our research staff about employment opportunities in their fields. This book would not have been possible without their assistance. Our thanks, too, to Catalyst, which has one of the best career libraries in the country in its New York, NY, offices, and to the National Society for Internships and Experiential Education, Raleigh, NC, which provided information on internship opportunities for a variety of professions. The following individuals and organizations were particularly generous with their time and evaluations of the information contained in this book:

Lynn Jones, Postgraduate Center for Mental Health
J.R. Wible, Jr., American Society for Personnel Adminstration

CAREER ASSOCIATES

Senior Editor—Series Development:	Peggy J. Schmidt
Project Editor:	M. J. Territo
Series Editorial Assistant:	Alan Selsor
Editors:	Ruth Cavin Jill Gorham
Researchers-Writers:	Jane Collins Kim Larsen Barbara Milton Alan Selsor
Researchers:	Fletcher Harper Deirdre Swords Martha Sutro

Series Concept Created by Ramsey Walker

CONTENTS

WHAT'S IN THIS BOOK FOR YOU?

ADVERTISING 1

- Creative 5
- Media 7
- Research 9
- Account Services 11
- Interviews 18

DEPARTMENT STORE RETAILING 21

- Store Management 25
- Buying 27
- Interviews 33

EDUCATION 37

- Teaching 43
- Interviews 49

HUMAN SERVICES 53

- Counseling 58
- Psychology Paraprofessional 59
- Administration 60
- Advocacy 61
- Research 62
- Community Relations 63
- Program Development 64
- Interviews 69

MARKET RESEARCH 73

- Research Analysis 77
- Interviews 83

PERSONNEL 87

Employment and Recruitment 91
Compensation and Benefits 93
Employee/Labor Relations 96
Interviews 101

PUBLIC RELATIONS 105

The Work 111
Interviews 119

REAL ESTATE 123

Sales 128
Appraisal 131
Property Management 133
Interviews 140

BIBLIOGRAPHY

INDEX

WHAT'S IN THIS BOOK FOR YOU?

Recent college graduates, no matter what their major has been, too often discover that there is a dismaying gap between their knowledge and planning and the reality of an actual career. Possibly even more unfortunate is the existence of potentially satisfying careers that graduates do not even know about. Although advice from campus vocational counselors, family, friends, and fellow students can be extremely helpful, there is no substitute for a structured exploration of the various alternatives open to graduates.

The Career Choices Series was created to provide you with the means to conduct such an exploration. It gives you specific, up-to-date information about the entry-level job opportunities in a variety of industries relevant to your degree and highlights opportunities that might otherwise be overlooked. Through its many special features—such as sections on internships, qualifications, and working conditions—the Career Choices Series can help you find out where your interests and abilities lie in order to point your search for an entry-level job in a productive direction. This book cannot find you a job—only you can provide the hard work, persistence, and ingenuity that that requires—but it can save you valuable time and energy. By helping you to narrow the range of your search to careers that are truly suitable for you, this book can help make hunting for a job an exciting adventure rather than a dreary—and sometimes frightening—chore.

The book's easy-to-use format combines general information about each of the industries covered with the hard facts that job-hunters must have. An overall explanation of each industry is followed by authoritative material on the job outlook for entry-level candidates, the competition for the openings that exist, and the new opportunities that may arise from such factors as expansion and technological development. There is a listing of employers by type and by geographic location and a sampling of leading companies by name—by no means all, but enough to give you a good idea of who the employers are.

The section on how to break into the field is not general how-to-get-a-job advice, but rather zeroes in on ways of getting a foot in the door of a particular industry.

You will find the next section, a description of the major functional areas within each industry, especially valuable in making your initial job choice. For example, communications majors aiming for magazine work can evaluate the editorial end, advertising space sales, circulation, or production. Those interested in accounting are shown the differences between management, government, and public accounting. Which of the various areas described offers you the best chance of an entry-level job? What career paths are likely to follow from that position? Will they help you reach your ultimate career goal? The sooner you have a basis to make the decision, the better prepared you can be.

For every industry treated and for the major functional areas within that industry, you'll learn what your duties—both basic and more challenging—are likely to be, what hours you'll work, what your work environment will be, and what range of salary to expect*. What personal and professional qualifications must you have? How can you move up—and to what? This book tells you.

You'll learn how it is possible to overcome the apparent contradiction of the truism, "To get experience you have to have experience." The kinds of extracurricular activities and work experience—summer and/or part-time—that can help you get and perform a job in your chosen area are listed. Internships are another way to get over that hurdle, and specific information is included for each industry. But you should also know that the directories published by the National Society for Internships and Experiential Education (Second Floor, 124 St. Mary's Street, Raleigh, NC 27605) are highly detailed and very useful. They are: *Directory of Undergraduate Internships, Directory of Washington Internships,* and *Directory of Public Service Internships*.

You'll find a list of the books and periodicals you should read to keep up with the latest trends in an industry you're considering,

---

* Salary figures given are the latest available as the book goes to press.

and the names and addresses of professional associations that can be helpful to you—through student chapters, open meetings, and printed information. Finally, interviews with professionals in each field bring you the experiences of people who are actually working in the kinds of jobs you may be aiming for.

Although your entry-level job neither guarantees nor locks you into a lifelong career path, the more you know about what is open to you, the better chance you'll have for a rewarding work future. The information in these pages will not only give you a realistic basis for a good start, it will help you immeasurably in deciding what to explore further on your own. So good reading, good hunting, good luck, and the best of good beginnings.

ADVERTISING

ARE you someone who spends as much time looking at the ads in a magazine as at the editorial sections? Do you find yourself wondering how effective certain television jingles are? Are you more interested in finding out who won a Clio than who won a Tony or an Oscar? If you answer yes, or if you even know what a Clio is, chances are you're a good candidate for a career in advertising.

Advertising agencies hire people from a wide variety of backgrounds—liberal arts, communications, business, and psychology among them—because jobs requiring different skills exist in the four major departments:

- **Creative**
- **Media**
- **Research**
- **Account Services**

At most agencies, the greatest number of jobs can be found in the creative department, where ads are written (and designed by people with a visual arts background) and the media department, which deals with planning a marketing strategy and buying air time and space in printed media for the agency's ads. As a copywriter, your communications or English degree will matter less than your actual speaking and writing skills. It is important to be an idea person, able to come up with many approaches to describe a product. If you want to go into media, ease with numbers is a must.

Research, which studies consumers' perceptions of products and advertising effectiveness, also hires entry-level people from a variety of disciplines, although a solid statistical background is a real asset. You must be able to read and interpret data, and have a real interest in the products and consumer reactions to them.

Account Services, where people work hand-in-hand with the clients, is reserved for those who have already gained experience in the industry, and it's the most direct link with clients and a path to management positions. The media department is the surest route to the account group, although some researchers end up there as well. Some large agencies rotate promising candidates through the media, research, and traffic departments on the way to account services.

Although there is good money to be made in advertising at big agencies, the advertising industry offers less security than many media professions. When an agency loses a major client, those who worked on that account are often let go. If enough income is lost, additional cuts may be made in areas not directly involved. Because client satisfaction is paramount, everyone who works at an agency—from top management to department heads to assistants—feels the pressure of getting work out when the client requests it. That often means staying late to make sure that the copy or reports or recommendations are the best job possible given the time constraints the client has set.

Technological advances are increasing the advertising industry's efficiency and organization. More and more research and account people are using microcomputers, for example. New areas for advertising, like cable television and videotex (described below) are creating more opportunities to expand an agency's services.

Job Outlook

Job Openings Will Grow: As fast as average

Competition for Jobs: Keen

New Job Opportunities: One of the hottest new advertising outlets is videotex, an interactive system that connects a keyboard terminal in a viewer's home to a central computer that broadcasts printed matter over telephone wires. The first such system (called Viewtron) began service in the Miami area in 1983 and brought subscribers hot-off-the-wire news and teleservices, such as banking, local restaurant menus, and shopping information.

Geographic Job Index

New York, NY, is the home of major ad agencies, the headquarters of the media and many Fortune 1000 firms, each of which also has an advertising department of its own. Chicago, IL, Los Angeles, CA, and Detroit, MI, are the next largest advertising centers. The advertising industry is growing faster than average in Atlanta, GA, Dallas, TX, and Houston, TX.

Who the Employers Are

ADVERTISING AGENCIES in the United States number more than 6000. Nearly all major advertising is created within agencies, where the vast majority of jobs are. Most agencies are small, but about a third are large organizations, some employing more than 1000 people.

IN-HOUSE AGENCIES can be found at large companies. In-house agencies provide anything from specialized functions to the full range of marketing services, some of which exceed what full-service agencies offer. Packaged-goods companies rely on independent agencies for most of their work, with the exception of TV network placement. Although responsibilities and salaries are comparable to those in independent agencies, there is less competition for creative jobs in corporate environments.

Major Employers

ADVERTISING AGENCIES

BBDO International, Inc., New York, NY
D'Arcy-MacManus & Masius, Inc., New York, NY
Doyle Dane Bernbach International, Inc., New York, NY
Foote, Cone & Belding, Chicago, IL
J. Walter Thompson Company, New York, NY
Leo Burnett Company, Inc., Chicago, IL
McCann-Erickson Worldwide, New York, NY
Ogilvy & Mather, Inc., New York, NY
SSC&B, Inc., New York, NY
Saatchi, Saatchi and Compton, Inc., New York, NY
Ted Bates Worldwide, Inc., New York, NY
Young & Rubicam, Inc., New York, NY

How to Break into the Field

Talent, persistence, assertiveness, and enthusiasm are particularly important ingredients in the job campaign of a would-be ad person. If you cannot creatively and imaginatively sell yourself, chances are you won't be good at selling ideas and products to the public—and employers are quick to sense that.

Large agencies are often in contact with the placement directors at a select number of colleges, so it pays to check with that office on your campus. Large companies with their own in-house agencies sometimes recruit on college campuses. But more often than not, it will be up to you to set up interviews on your own. Find out all you can about the agencies at the top of your list (alumni who work there are often good sources of information).

To land a job in the creative department, you need a portfolio of your writing and ideas. It can include your best work on the school paper or radio or TV station. It's less important that your work was published or used commercially than that it shows originality and imagination.

While portfolios aren't necessary for jobs in the other three major departments, sensitivity to and interest in contemporary tastes and trends and some knowledge of the various media are.

CREATIVE

Writing copy requires a feeling for the language that goes beyond the simple communication of information. Rhythm, syntax, and meaning influence the choice of words that will create the right mood and reaction. Copywriters are well paid for their talent, since their command of the language can move millions to purchase a product. In fact, television commercial copywriters earn more money per word than any other kind of writer.

The best way to break into any agency—large or small—is to show that you're a good idea person who is able to come up with clever phrases, catchy slogans, and eye-catching copy. As a junior copywriter, you will be working as a member of a creative team under the supervision of a more experienced copywriter. You may be expected to write copy for a campaign, or you may have to come up with some original ideas for selling a product or service. Depending on the size of the agency and the importance of the campaign, you may be invited to take part in brainstorming sessions, where a group of creative people toss out ideas for a new campaign.

Qualifications

Personal: Good interpersonal skills. A good imagination. Persuasiveness. A strong enough ego to withstand frequent criticism. Sensitivity to current trends. Enormous enthusiasm. Ability to work under pressure.

Professional: Strong language and writing skills. Knowledge of the media.

Career Paths

LEVEL	JOB TITLE	EXPERIENCE NEEDED
Entry	Junior copywriter	College degree
2	Copywriter	1-3 years
3	Senior copywriter	7-10 years
4	Copy chief	10+ years

Job Responsibilities

Entry Level

THE BASICS: Learning about the client or clients from printed material and past correspondence. In small agencies: Answering the phone. Typing. Filing. Drafting simple correspondence.

MORE CHALLENGING DUTIES: Writing descriptive copy. Coming up with concepts for new ad campaigns. Working with the art department on presentations.

Moving Up

Your success will be linked to the success of your creative group at a large agency; at a small one, your effectiveness depends directly on your own contribution. Promotions will be based on your consistently good ideas and great copy. Moving up may mean getting a more significant role to play on a national account or being switched to a more prestigious client. With several years' experience and a solid track record, you may become a supervisor of other copywriters and work with the media and account groups developing ad campaign concepts.

MEDIA

A sound strategy for the placement of ads is the job of media planners, who must reduce quantities of raw numerical material to arrive at the most cost-effective way of reaching potential buyers.

As an assistant, you'll be assigned to work on an account under the supervision of a more experienced planner. In big agencies, as many as 25 to 30 people from the four major groups (account, creative, research, and media) may be involved in the media planning process, although you'll work primarily with the account services people. Developing a media strategy involves studying the target audience, geography (where customers live), seasonality of a product, reach and frequency (the distribution of ads and how often they should run), and creative considerations (such as the tone of the ad).

You'll spend considerable time using computers and VisiCalc programs, which speed up routine computation. You'll be analyzing research about the product and its customers or potential customers and extracting usable data from such numbers as the CPM (cost per thousand), the cost of reaching 1000 people in the target audience, and the GRP (gross rating points), the number of people reached for a certain expenditure.

Coming up with the right media mix is challenging because there are so many options. Although you'll know the budget the client has allocated for advertising, the media group may well recommend a higher or lower figure.

Once the client approves the media plan, buyers execute the decisions. In small agencies, planning and buying are often done by the same people, but in the larger ones the tasks are separate. Buyers are more marketing and sales-oriented, and negotiation is a big part of their job. Regional spot buyers, who buy air time on regional radio and television, usually aspire to be network spot buyers, because these buyers handle the most expensive advertising purchases of all.

Qualifications

Personal: Strong interpersonal skills. Ability to work as a member of a team. Good judgment. Willingness to assume responsibility for decisions.

Professional: Basic math skills. Ability to make oral presentations to groups. Strong writing skills.

Career Paths

LEVEL	JOB TITLE	EXPERIENCE NEEDED
Entry	Assistant media planner	College degree
2	Media planner	3-5 years
3	Associate media director	5-7 years
4	Media director of planning	7-10 years
5	Media manager of planning and buying	10+ years

Job Responsibilities

Entry Level

THE BASICS: Learning to interpret rate cards of various media. Heavy computation. Doing work sheets. Analyzing audience ratings (such as Nielsen ratings). Writing letters and memos.

MORE CHALLENGING DUTIES: Comparing media alternatives. Preparing for and delivering presentations to clients. Talking to sales representatives from various media. Evaluating media buys.

Moving Up

Although you must demonstrate basic competence with numbers, your promotability largely depends on selling your ideas about a particular campaign both to members of the team and, most important, to the client. Being able to handle pressure and crises will also help you land a place on interesting and challenging accounts. The most desirable ones are packagedgoods accounts, because these clients invest a lot of money in advertising and demand quality service. After three years on packaged-goods accounts, you can often move into account services. Those who enjoy media planning stay on to become managers in that department if they demonstrate talent and administrative skills.

RESEARCH

The research department is the center of market analysis, consumer research, product evaluation, and concept testing—all the considerations that go into the formulation of a marketing strategy or an advertising campaign.

As an entry-level person, your main responsibilities will be to gather and organize data for the more experienced people in the department. You may be doing primary research—designing surveys to test a hypothesis about a particular product or the consumers who may buy it. In addition to deciding what kinds of questions should be asked and their format, you also pinpoint who the survey respondents should be and how they should be questioned. Once you've worked out all the details, you'll hand over the task of actually carrying out the survey to an outside "supplier," a market research firm. The supplier will present you with a summary of the research results, often rows and columns of numbers. Research analysts figure out what patterns and trends the numbers signify and how they should affect the marketing and advertising campaign.

Secondary research involves culling information published by the government, the trade, or other groups. You'll write reports summarizing the results, which may be used by the creative, account services, or media people.

Before an advertising campaign is created and implemented, the key issue researchers focus on is the consumer's perception of a particular product. Once the campaign is executed, the important thing to determine is whether the advertising is being correctly perceived by those for whom it is intended.

Qualifications

Personal: Problem-solving mentality. A logical, analytical mind. Ability to work independently, yet contribute to a team effort. Good organizational skills.

Professional: Good writing skills. Ability to work with statistics. Familiarity with data interpretation.

Career Paths

LEVEL	JOB TITLE	EXPERIENCE NEEDED
Entry	Project director	College or graduate degree. One year of market research experience preferred.
2	Research account executive	1-3 years
3	Associate research director	3-8 years
4	Research director	7-10 years
5	Department manager	10+ years

Job Responsibilities

Entry Level

THE BASICS: Plenty of paperwork. Posting numbers from computer printouts. Researching printed literature.

MORE CHALLENGING DUTIES: Drafting reports from research. Getting competitive bids from suppliers. Sitting in on planning sessions. Suggesting new methods of data gathering. Helping design surveys.

Moving Up

Demonstrating that you are a talented interpreter of the information you collect is critical in getting promoted, as is coming up with innovative ways to test product information, advertising strategy, or new markets. The more you are able to contribute to the success of a campaign, the more likely it is your star will rise quickly. If, on top of talents for research and analysis, you prove to be an adroit decision-maker, you can move into a management position. Research can also be a pathway to jobs in the account and media groups for those who are more business-oriented.

ACCOUNT SERVICES

Account executives serve as the link between the agency and the client. They oversee all aspects of an ad campaign, working with all other departments to make sure that problems are solved, that work is completed on time, and that everyone involved knows his or her responsibilities. The creative department looks to the account executive for information about the product and for help in creating campaign ideas. Those in research need direction to determine what information is needed about the product and its potential consumers. The media group works closely with the account executives to develop the best marketing strategy and media mix possible for the amount of money budgeted.

The client relies on the account executive to answer questions, correct misunderstandings, and take care of mistakes. Keeping a client happy can involve hand-holding, pacifying, reassuring, and being available for frequent consultations, while not neglecting other clients or the development of new prospects. Profitability is the bottom-line concern of account executives. Given that financial responsibility, two or more years of experience in the business is usually a prerequisite for a job, although some large agencies train particularly qualified candidates. If you were a business major in college and have worked as an intern or summer employee in product development for a major consumer goods manufacturer or in account services in an advertising agency, you may be considered for such a training program.

Qualifications

Personal: Good judgment. Strong interpersonal skills. Willingness to be on the firing line. Sensitivity to current trends. Leadership qualities.

Professional: Negotiation skills. Advertising or marketing experience. Knowledge of product development and manufacturing. Sales acumen.

Career Paths

LEVEL	JOB TITLE	EXPERIENCE NEEDED
Entry	Account executive trainee	College degree. Advertising-related experience.
2	Account executive	1-3 years
3	Senior account executive	5-8 years
4	Accounts supervisor or manager	10-13 years

Job Responsibilities

Entry Level

THE BASICS: Fielding material from other departments. Taking calls from clients. Keeping in touch with the traffic department on schedules for ads and spots. Monitoring deadlines and pressing creative people for overdue copy. Following through on any marketing needs.

MORE CHALLENGING DUTIES: Meeting with clients. Participating in meetings with other departments. Consulting with the creative department on the ideas for a campaign. Planning an overall strategy for your client. Keeping up-to-date on media rate changes and new media outlets.

Moving Up

Once you demonstrate that you're able to deal effectively with clients and work well with your colleagues in other departments, you'll be given a bigger role on a major account or possibly one or two small accounts of your own. (Even newcomers work on major accounts taking care of all the details for more senior account executives.) It is your responsibility to anticipate and prevent potential problems and confrontations while doing your best for both the agency and the client. Building a successful record of ad campaigns and developing a reputation for being easy to work with can eventually earn you the title of senior account executive.

Only those who are effective managers and have well-honed administrative skills eventually become account managers and supervisors, overseeing and nurturing a number of accounts and going after new business. They hold regular meetings with their sales group to point out prospects and build up a file of potential clients, and they engineer the agency pitch for new business.

ADDITIONAL INFORMATION

Salaries

The trade magazine *Adweek* does an annual salary survey. The following figures, which represent the national median annual salary for each position, are take from the July 1983 issue:

CREATIVE	
Copywriter	$25,200
Creative director	$50,000
MEDIA	
Media buyer	$16,000
Media planner	$20,000
Media department head	$34,500
RESEARCH	
Research services director	$35,000
ACCOUNT SERVICES	
Assistant account executive	$19,000
Account executive	$28,000
Account department head	$47,000

Working Conditions

Hours: Deadlines and emergencies are the normal course of business at most agencies. Clients must be satisfied, which often means putting in evening or weekend hours, depending on the pressure your department is under to produce.

Environment: Entry-level people in all departments often work in bullpens, but they generally share an office with one or two others. More experienced people have their own offices—and more privacy. Account people usually rate the most attractive office space because they meet with clients and are responsible for millions of dollars in billing.

Workstyle: Creative, media, and account people spend a lot of time in meetings and presentations—with each other and with clients. When you're not discussing ideas and strategies, you'll be at your desk—working over copy if you're in creative or working with figures if you're in media. Account execs spend a lot of time on the phone with clients. Research staff spend their time designing surveys and working with outside market research firms. The media staff gets a coveted perk—lots of lunches paid for by the media sales representatives.

Travel: Travel opportunities vary according to client needs, your position within the agency, and the size of the account, but, generally speaking, most work is done at the agency.

Extracurricular Activities/Work Experience

Campus newspaper or TV or radio station—writing, editing, space sales

Student-run business (or your own)—promoting, marketing, and selling a product or service

Market research firms—working as an intern or summer employee

Internships

The American Advertising Federation offers a variety of internship possibilities through its members nationwide. The scope of each program and the requirements vary from sponsor to sponsor. A complete list of members, which includes companies with in-house advertising departments and agencies, is available by writing to the American Advertising Federation. Interested students must inquire directly with sponsors, keeping in mind that not all members take interns.

Recommended Reading

BOOKS

Ayer Glossary of Advertising and Related Terms, Ayer Press: 1977

Blood, Brains, and Beer: An Autobiography by David Ogilvy, Atheneum Publishers: 1978

Confessions of an Advertising Man by David Ogilvy, Antheneum Publishers: 1980

How to Put Your Book Together and Get a Job in Advertising by Maxine Paetro, E.P. Dutton: 1980

Madison Avenue Handbook by Peter Glenn Publications, Ltd.: 1983

New Advertising: Twenty-one Successful Campaigns from Avis to Volkswagen by Robert Glatzer, Citadel Press: 1970

Ogilvy on Advertising by David Olgilvy, Crown Publishers: 1979

Roster and Organization of the American Association of Advertising Agencies: 1982-3 (available free from AAAA)

Standard Directory of Advertising Agencies (Agency Red Book), National Register Publishing Company: 1983

PERIODICALS

Advertising Age (weekly), Crain Communications, Inc., 740 North Rush Street, Chicago, IL 60611

Adweek (weekly), Adweek Publications, 820 Second Avenue, New York, NY 10017 (regional editions for East, Southeast, West, Southwest, and Midwest)

Professional Associations

The Advertising Council
825 Third Avenue
New York, NY 10022

Advertising Research Foundation
Information Center
3 East 54th Street
New York, NY 10022

American Advertising Federation
1400 K Street, N.W.
Suite 1000
Washington, DC 20005

American Association of Advertising Agencies
200 Park Avenue
New York, NY 10017

Association of National Advertisers
155 East 44th Street
New York, NY 10017

INTERVIEWS

Susan Montgomery, Age 33
Copywriter
Wells, Rich and Green, Inc., New York, NY

Before I became a copywriter, I worked as a secretary in an ad agency. That's not a prerequisite to a job; it's how I happened to start my career. A friend who worked in the creative department suggested that I could make a lot more money writing copy than typing it. So I went to a school called The Advertising Center in Los Angeles, where I learned advertising concepts, copywriting, and how to put together a portfolio of sample ads. I then went around to various agencies in Los Angeles, but my ad agency friend suggested that if I were really serious about my career, I should go to New York. So I did.

I quickly discovered that when you have a portfolio to show, people are very willing to talk to you. I hardly knew anyone and just began knocking on the doors of various agencies. That's the way to get interviewed. Six weeks after I arrived I was hired by Well, Rich and Green, Inc. If your book is good, sooner or later you'll get a job.

Although I have a degree in English and my education has been useful, my portfolio won me my job. Creative directors are always looking for people who can come up with fresh ideas and solutions to advertising problems. And you have to be able to deal with the people you're working with, who can be difficult at times.

For a person interested in writing, copywriting can be a lucrative way to make a living; however, job security is often out of your control. And losing your job may have nothing to do with you or your work. If the agency loses a big account, a lot of people can be fired because the agency may have supported more people than actually worked on that particular account. That possibility is frightening to some people, but it really doesn't bother me that much.

That's why it's important, throughout your career, to do the best work you can. If that quality is reflected in your portfolio, it won't be long before you're hired.

Al Paul Lefton, Jr., Age 55
President, Chief Executive Officer
Al Paul Lefton Company, Inc., Philadelphia, PA

I started in advertising in 1950 after graduating from Yale. Yale had a divisional major called Sociology, History, and Literature, which I found to be very helpful, especially the sociology courses.

I interview starting-level people. Good grades and the ability to write well and express oneself clearly are essential. The particular academic major is not especially important, but it has to have something to do with words—journalism, English literature, liberal arts.

I would recommend that you do something to make your application different from all the others. I get hundreds of résumés that all look the same. Of course, if the pages are stapled out of order, if postage is due or if the cover letter has misspellings (I get a lot where my name is misspelled!), they go right into the wastebasket.

I am not impressed by gratuitous compliments about our agency that I know are being made about every other agency. I look for applications that show that the writer has done some research, perhaps about a new account we have or that offer some pertinent and interesting observation about a current one.

In the interview, I look for a very high degree of interpersonal skills, fair-mindedness, and balance, for someone who is a good strategist and has a sense of drama and attention to details.

Entry-level positions in advertising often involve a lot of clerical work. The next step on the business side is to an assistant's post, quite often in media or account service. This type of job involves a lot of paperwork and very little decision-making, but it provides the opportunity to learn from firsthand experience. At the next step, account executive, you begin to have some autonomy. It is at this level that you either sink or swim. You have the responsibility for properly servicing an account and making it grow. If you prove to be competent and skillful, you advance to the next level, account supervisor, and beyond that to management supervisor.

Is there security in the agency business? Well, it clearly does not provide the security of a government job. But for all the challenges and diversity of assignments, there have to be risks.

Our industry has gone through remarkable increases in productivity. Twenty years ago, it used to take nine people to handle a million dollars in billings. It now takes only three people per million dollars, and that figure will decline further with increased use of computers, which we now use heavily in testing media schedules and doing in-house typography. Like most fields, advertising has its highs and lows. During those periods when you have to get ready for a sales meeting or put together a presentation which is crucial to the growth of new business, you simply have to postpone your social life. But what I like most about advertising is that you don't do the same thing on any given day. There is always a different kind of client problem to solve.

DEPARTMENT STORE RETAILING

CONSUMERS generally take for granted that they will always find their favorite department stores brimming with merchandise. Unnoticed by most customers, a large, talented staff works long, hard hours to keep the shelves filled, the selection varied, the stores beautiful, and the business of retailing running smoothly. Retailing is an industry in which brains and diligence can take you to high levels of decision-making years before your contemporaries in other fields have reached similar positions of responsibility.

Graduates of virtually any discipline may enter department store retailing. Prospective employers are looking for demonstrated capacity to learn and make quick, sound judgments and are less interested in academic backgrounds. You must be flexible, comfortable with people, self-disciplined, and highly motivated—and a sense of humor certainly does not hurt. Retailing is a high-pressure profession where no slow seasons exist—only busy and busier, with the November-December pre-Christmas rush being the most hectic time of all. Prior retail experience, even a summer spent behind a cash register, is a plus; some retailers won't consider candidates without it.

Most entry-level jobs are in merchandising, an area further divided into:

- **Store Management**
- **Buying**

Your job in merchandising begins with a training period of six months to a year. Some trainees divide their time between classroom learning and work experience, others train entirely on the job. Generally, the larger the retailer, the more formalized the training. Whether you enter the field via store management or buying depends primarily on the employer. Many stores separate these functions beginning at the entry level; you must choose which path you prefer. Other stores will introduce all new merchandising personnel to buying and later allow those interested in and qualified for management to move up. The opposite arrangement, moving into buying at some later stage, also occurs, although infrequently.

The modern store is reaping the benefits of the technological revolution. Point-of-sale computer terminals are replacing mechanical cash registers; these automatically compute sales, taxes, and discounts and simplify inventory control by keeping sales records. Computers are also used for credit records and tracking sales forecasts.

Retailing is vulnerable to downturns in the economy, but it's one of the first industries to bounce back after a recession. As a highly profit-oriented business, it's hectic and competitive. The customer's satisfaction and loyalty to the store are very important, which means that you must tolerate and even pamper people whom you may not like. In retailing, the unexpected is the order of the day; you can expect to feel pressured, but seldom unchallenged.

Job Outlook

Job Openings Will Grow: As fast as average

Competition for Jobs: Keen
In merchandising, the most competition exists in buying; this area has fewer openings, tends to pay a bit better, and has an aura of glamour about it.

New Job Opportunities: An exciting new technological development, still in experimental form, that may change retailing in the next decade is video retailing. A select number of communities now have a two-way cable television system through which viewers may receive and send information to a broadcasting center. Viewers can order goods seen on the screen by typing their selections on a keyboard. Video retailing is still in developmental form, but those entering retailing should be aware of its potential as a new job area.

Geographic Job Index

The location of retail jobs parallels the distribution of the general population; stores operate where customers live. As an up-and-coming executive in a retail chain, expect to work in a city or suburban area. Most new store construction in the coming years is expected to take place in revitalizing city cores. Department stores are found across the country, with the highest concentration of jobs in the Northeast, Midwest and West Coast.

If your interest is buying, your geographic options are more limited. For many department store chains, most or all buying takes place in a few key markets, notably New York, NY.

Who the Employers Are

A retailer is, in its simplest definition, a third party who sells a producer's goods to a consumer for a profit. The retailing industry as a whole comprises a wide variety of stores of different sizes with different personnel needs. Management personnel are sought by all major retail firms, including grocery, drug, specialty, and variety store chains, but because the most varied opportunities are found in department stores, this chapter focuses on this sector of retailing.

Major Employers

Allied Stores Corporation, New York, NY
- Bonwit Teller
- Field's
- Jordan Marsh
- Stern's

Carter Hawley Hale Stores, Los Angeles, CA
- Bergdorf Goodman
- The Broadway
- John Wanamaker
- Neiman-Marcus

Dayton Hudson Corporation, Minneapolis, MN
- Dayton's
- Diamond's

Federated Department Stores, New York, NY
- Abraham & Straus
- Bullock's
- Filene's
- Foley's
- I. Magnin
- Rich's

R.H. Macy & Company, New York, NY

Montgomery Ward & Company, Chicago, IL

J. C. Penney Company, New York, NY

Sears, Roebuck & Company, Chicago, IL

How to Break into the Field

Your best bet is on-campus interviews. Major retailers actively recruit on college campuses. This is the most accessible way to most potential employers. Don't hesitate, however, to contact employers directly, especially if you want to work for a smaller operation. Read the business section of your newspaper regularly to find out about store expansions, the addition of new stores or locations, and other developments in retailing that can provide important clues to new job openings. Keep in mind that retail or selling experience of any kind will increase your chances of getting hired.

International Job Opportunities

Extremely limited. Opportunities to live abroad exist at the corporate level of a few international chains.

STORE MANAGEMENT

If you're a "people person," consider the store management side of merchandising. You'll be responsible for handling the needs of staff and customers.

The job of store management personnel, even at entry level, entails making decisions on your own. But since decisions often have to be made on the spot and involve balancing the interests of both customers and the store, your mistakes are likely to be highly visible. Whether you manage the smallest department or a very large store, you must always keep the bottom line—making a profit—in mind when making decisions.

During training, you will work with experienced managers and will be moved throughout the store to observe all aspects of merchandising. If you're quick to learn and demonstrate management potential, you'll soon be made manager of a small department or assistant manager of a large one. You will have a fair amount of autonomy, but you must stick to store standards and implement policies determined by higher level management.

Qualifications

Personal: Ability to learn quickly. Enormous enthusiasm. The flexibility to handle a constantly changing schedule. Willingness to work weekends, holidays, and nights.

Professional: Demonstrated leadership ability. Ability to work with figures, finances, inventories, and quotas. A sense of diplomacy.

Career Paths

LEVEL	JOB TITLE	EXPERIENCE NEEDED
Entry	Department manager trainee	College degree
2	Group department manager	2-3 years
3	Assistant store manager	5-10 years
4	Store manager	8-12 years

Job Responsibilities

Entry Level

THE BASICS: Handling staff scheduling. Dealing with customer complaints. Doing plenty of paperwork.

MORE CHALLENGING DUTIES: Monitoring and motivating your sales staff. Assisting in the selection of merchandise for your department. Making decisions and solving problems.

Moving Up

Advancement in store management depends on how well you shoulder responsibility and take advantage of opportunities to learn. Effectively leading your staff, moving merchandise, and, above all, turning a profit will secure your promotion into higher levels.

Your first management position will be overseeing a small department, handling greater volumes of money and merchandise. The group department manager directs several department managers, coordinating store operations on a larger scale. From here you might progress to assistant store manager and store manager; this last position is, in many respects, similar to running a private business. The best may then go on to the corporate level.

Relocation is often necessary in order to win promotions. Switching store locations every three years or so is not uncommon. However, depending on the chain, a change of workplace need not require a change of address; often stores are within easy driving distance of each other. But the larger the chain, the greater the possibility that you'll have to move to a different city to further your career.

BUYING

Do you fantasize about a shopping spree in the world's fashion capitals? A few lucky buyers, after years of work and experience, are paid to do just that when they're sent to Hong Kong, Paris, or Milan to select new lines of merchandise. Most do not make it to such heights, but on a smaller scale, this is the business of buying.

A buyer decides which goods will be available in a store. Buyers authorize merchandise purchases from wholesalers and set the retail prices. A sensitivity to changing trends, tastes, and styles and an ability to understand and forecast the preference of your own store's customers is crucial. Buyers must also maintain standards of quality while keeping within certain ranges of affordability.

The buyer who works for a discount department store faces a particularly tough job. Obtaining lower-than-average prices for quality merchandise is a real challenge and requires an unerring eye and an ability to negotiate with sellers.

Astute buying translates into profits for the store and advancement for your career. Learning how to spend large sums of money wisely takes practice. Fortunately, as a new buyer you can afford to make a few mistakes, even an occasional expensive one, without jeopardizing your career. A good buyer takes calculated risks, and as you gain experience more of your choices will succeed.

During training, you'll work immediately as an assistant to an experienced buyer. The trainee progresses by observing, asking questions, and offering to take on appropriate responsibilities.

Qualifications

Personal: An interest in changing trends and fashions. An ability to work with a wide variety of personalities. A willingness to channel creativity into a commercial enterprise.

Professional: Financial and negotiating know-how. Organizational skills. Good judgment in spotting trends and evaluating products.

Career Paths

LEVEL	JOB TITLE	EXPERIENCE NEEDED
Entry	Assistant or junior buyer	College degree and store training
2	Buyer (small lines)	2-5 years
3	Buyer (large lines)	4-10 years
4	Corporate merchandise manager	15+ years

Job Responsibiiities

Entry Level

THE BASICS: Assisting your supervising buyer. Placing orders and speaking with manufacturers by phone. Supervising the inspection and unpacking of new merchandise and overseeing its distribution.

MORE CHALLENGING DUTIES: Becoming acquainted with various manufacturers' lines. Considering products for purchase. Evaluating your store's needs. Keeping an eye on the competition.

Moving Up

Advancement depends on proof of your ability to judge customer needs and to choose saleable goods. The only purchases closely scrutinized by higher authorities are those inconsistent with past practices and standards.

After completing your training, you will first buy for a small department, then, as you become seasoned, for larger departments. High-placed buyers make decisions in buying for a key department common to several stores, for an entire state, or possibly for many stores. Your buying plans must always be well coordinated with the needs of store management.

ADDITIONAL INFORMATION

Salaries

Entry-level salaries range from $12,000 to $18,000 a year, depending on the employer and the geographic location of the store. Junior buyers tend to be among the best paid entry-level employees.

The following salary ranges show typical annual salaries for experienced retail personnel. In merchandising salaries vary with the size and importance of your department.

2-4 years:	$16,000-24,000
5-10 years:	$22,000-27,000
12 years or more:	$25,000 and up

Working Conditions

Hours: Most retail personnel work a five-day, 40-hour week, but schedules vary with different positions. In store management, daily shifts are rarely nine to five, because stores are open as many as 12 hours a day, seven days a week. Night, weekend, and holiday duty are unavoidable, especially for newcomers. Operations personnel work similar hours. Buyers have more regular schedules and are rarely asked to work evening and weekend hours.

Environment: In merchandising, your time is divided between the office and the sales floor—more often the latter. Office space at the entry level may or may not be private, depending on the store. Whether you share space or not, expect to be close to the sales floor. Merchandising is no place for those who need absolute privacy and quiet in order to be productive.

Workstyle: In store management, office time is 100 percent work; every valuable moment must be used effectively to keep on top of the paperwork. On the floor you will be busy overseeing the arrangement of merchandise, meeting with your sales staff, and listening to customer complaints. Long hours on your feet will test your patience and endurance, but you can never let the weariness show. In buying, office time is spent with paperwork and calls to manufacturers. You might also review catalog copy and illustrations. On the sales floor, you'll meet with store personnel to see how merchandise is displayed and, most important, to see how the customers are responding. Manufacturers' representatives will visit to show their products, and you might spend some days at manufacturer and wholesaler showrooms. Because these jobs bring you into the public eye, you must be well dressed and meticulously groomed. The generous discounts that employees receive as a fringe benefit help defray the cost of maintaining a wardrobe.

Travel: In store management, your responsibility lies with your own department and your own store; travel opportunities are virtually nonexistent, except for some top-level personnel. Buyers, particularly those who live outside major manufacturing centers, may make annual trips to New York, NY, and other key cities. You might also travel to trade shows at which your type of merchandise is displayed.

Extracurricular Activities/Work Experience

Leadership in campus organizations

Treasurer or financial officer of an organization

Sales position on the yearbook or campus newspaper

Summer or part-time work in any aspect of retailing

Internships

Arrange internships with individual stores or chains; many are eager to hire interns, preferring students who are in the fall semester of their senior year. Check with your school's placement or internship office or with the store itself in the spring for a fall internship. Summer internships are also available with some stores. Contact the placement office or the personnel departments of individual stores for details.

Recommended Reading

BOOKS

Buyer's Manual, National Retail Merchants Association: 1979

Creative Selling: A Programmed Approach by R.J. Burley, Addison-Wesley: 1982

The Retail Revolution: Market Transformation, Investment, and Labor in the Modern Department Store by Barry Bluestone et al., Auburn House: 1981

The Woolworths by James Brough, McGraw-Hill: 1982

PERIODICALS

Advertising Age (weekly), Crain Communications, 740 North Rush Street, Chicago, IL 60611

Journal of Retailing (quarterly), New York University, 202 Tisch Building, New York, NY 10003

Stores (monthly), National Retail Merchants Association, 100 West 31st Street, New York, NY 10001

Women's Wear Daily (daily), Fairchild Publications, Inc., 7 East 12th Street, New York, NY 10003

Professional Associations

American Marketing Association
250 South Wacker Drive
Chicago, IL 60606

American Retail Federation
1616 H Street, N.W.
Washington, DC 20006

Association of General Merchandise Chains
1625 I Street, N.W.
Washington, DC 20006

National Retail Merchants Association
100 West 31st Street
New York, NY 10001

INTERVIEWS

Carolyn Egan, Age 33
Fashion Coordinator
Bloomingdale's Department Store, NY

My first job was far removed from retailing—I taught high school math for a year. But the school environment really didn't excite me and I felt I could get more from a job. I saw an ad for the position of fashion coordinator at a branch of Gimbels' department store. I wasn't planning a career in retailing, but because I kept up with fashion and felt I had a flair for it, I applied. I got the job and enjoyed the work, but that particular branch was not a high-caliber store, and after two years I was ready to move on.

I took a part-time job as an assistant manager at an Ann Taylor store, one of a chain selling women's clothing. At that time I was also going to school to finish an art degree. My job included store management and some limited buying. I wound up managing my own store, but because Ann Taylor has a small management staff, I felt there wasn't enough growth potential. I came to know the man who was doing store design for the chain. He was expanding his operations and needed help, so I went to work with him. I designed store interiors and fixtures, which gave me a whole new perspective on the industry. I have been lucky to see so many sides of retailing, but these job changes also required me to relocate.

When I moved into fashion coordination with Bloomingdale's about seven years ago, I finally found what I had been looking for—a high-powered, high-pressured environment. When I walk into the store each morning I feel that things are moving, happening. That's the fun of retailing.

My responsibility is to work with the buyers, helping them choose the right styles. After you've been in retailing a number of years, you know where fashion has been and you can see where it's going. You decide—really by making educated guesses—what the public will want a year from today. My job includes a lot of travel—usually eight or nine weeks a year. Where there are products abroad, we explore them. That's the only way to keep up with the competition.

In buying we speak of hundreds of dozens, so you must be volume-oriented. You ask, "What does our regular customer want to see?" Then you make a decision that has to be more right than wrong. I work with children's wear, a department that rarely sees radical changes in style. But there are always new trends in color and design, and new products.

One of the toughest parts of my job is training new buyers and helping with their first big buys. They are understandably nervous about spending several hundred thousand dollars. The fashion coordinator is one with buying experience. You offer better advice if you understand the pressure and monetary responsibility of the buyer's job.

Even though I'm in a creative area, business and financial concerns are of the highest importance. You must have a head for business in every retailing job. You want to find beautiful quality products, but if they don't sell, you've failed.

The one drawback to my job is advancement. My talents and experience are best used right where I am now. Unlike the buyers, I really have no place higher to go. But I enjoy my work. I suppose it's like being an artist, and how many artists are really appreciated?

G. G. Michelson, Age 58
Senior Vice President for External Affairs
R. H. Macy & Company, NY

My job is a rather unique one—it had never existed before and was tailored just for me. I represent the company in the community in its relationships with government, and in philanthropy. I was the senior vice president for personnel and labor relations in the New York division before moving into the corporate side about five years ago.

I was given this opportunity because of my long association and familiarity with the company and the business. We have a separate public relations department, and I don't interfere with their plans; rather, I am involved in considerations of corporate policy. For example, I handle difficult shareholder and community questions. We have a substantial philanthropy budget to work with. We want to spend this money creatively, but our charitable actions must be in line with our business decisions. We are primarily concerned with the communities in which our stores are located, because we recognize our obligation to those places in which we make our living.

I was quite young when I graduated from college, so I went on to law school to mature and get that valuable credential—but I never intended to practice law. All along I knew that I wanted to work in labor relations.

I considered manufacturing and some of the heavy industries as potential employers, and I came to realize that retailing as a service industry was far more people-intensive than other businesses. I found that in retailing the personnel function had a great deal more status and received more attention from top management. Looking elsewhere, I noticed that the emphasis was on cost control, not people development.

I went directly into Macy's training program from law school. The training program was and, of course, still is largely devoted to merchandising. I worked in merchandising only for the six months that I trained, but that experience gave me an excellent background for understanding the business and the people in it. In employee relations, I had responsibility for hiring, training, and developing our employees and merchandising talent.

In the past ten years, I have seen a significant change in the kind of graduates entering retailing. We now hire a great many graduates who once would have pursued other careers—graduates certified to teach, for instance—and people with liberal arts backgrounds who once would have gone on to grad school. We have always hired people who have broad educations; we have never been too concerned about a candidate's business background. We develop our talent by training people for top management, so we are looking for the ability to learn and grow. We don't want to have to train a person to think for the first time!

I spend a lot of time seeing and counseling young people who are investigating careers. My advice: be expansive and open to unforeseen opportunities. So many graduates have rigid plans—which I jokingly refer to as their "five-year plans." Often the best things that happen in a person's career development are totally unexpected. Bright people should be more flexible than many seem to be.

EDUCATION

MANY of the world's most prominent citizens have either started their careers as teachers or have added teaching to the list of their accomplishments. Leonardo da Vinci, Leo Tolstoy, Henry Kissinger, and Jimmy Carter are but a few.

Through the ages the theory of education has fascinated many. Tolstoy put off writing his novels in order to work out his ideas about education, and Plato devoted many of his philosophical treatises to exploring how knowledge is transmitted from teacher to student. People teach, he said, not by writing books or making speeches, but by becoming vitally involved in dialogue, in human relationships. Teaching is something that happens between two people; it is communication, knowledge passing from one to another.

Thousands of years later this still holds true. Ask almost any teacher what constitutes good teaching and he or she will tell you: good teaching is caring for the people you teach. There are less altruistic reasons for becoming a teacher, however, and if you ask a veteran, he or she will probably start with summer vacation—not to mention the three or four weeks of holidays that can accumulate at Christmas, Easter, Thanksgiving, and the scattered celebrations of America's heroes.

Teaching can often serve personal interests, too. For those who love to act, teaching provides the perfect audience. For those who like to be in charge, teaching is one of the few professions where you start off as the boss. For scholars, teaching is a way to delve further into your favorite subjects.

Of course, teaching is not the ideal state. Although the starting salaries can be commensurate with the job market as a whole, salaries for experienced teachers most definitely are not. Crime in the schools has received a lot of national coverage, but what is called crime by the media usually means discipline problems in the school, such as absenteeism, vandalism, and abuse of drugs or alcohol. But prospective teachers must take into account the disciplinary difficulties some of them will encounter.

Perhaps the most troubling problem facing a person interested in a teaching career is the beating teachers' reputations have taken in the last decade. As the quality of education seems to have gone steadily downward, largely because of factors beyond teachers' control, teachers themselves have had to take on more and more responsibilities—not only in the area of teaching, but in the area of genuine care and concern for their students.

Few professions, however, have more social significance than teaching, and none offers the sense of satisfaction that comes from contributing directly and positively to a young person's future. When Wally Schirra, one of the original seven U.S. astronauts, was asked who was the most influential person in his life, he didn't hesitate to say his second-grade teacher.

As computers become standard equipment in more and more classrooms, teacher applicants with computer skills are in a better position to be hired. The educational value of computers, however, depends on how teachers use them. The computer can be used as an automated taskmaster or, more importantly, as an interactive device. Some programs teach sophisticated skills such as thinking and writing even to very small children. Computers can grab and keep a student's attention, stimulate, and motivate him or her to higher levels of achievement. But it is still up to the teacher to provide the crucial interaction that makes learning possible.

Job Outlook

Job Openings Will: Decline

Competition For Jobs: Keen

New Job Opportunities: If current migration trends continue, a 25% decline in the number of 15 to 19-year-olds is projected in the northeast and north central states between 1980 and 1990. The rate of decline is expected to be 15% in the rest of the country. These statistics, combined with the fact that the 61,650 secondary school teacher applicants from the graduating class of 1981 exceeded the number of job openings by 18,150, indicate that new job opportunities are not plentiful. These statistics do not take into account, however, the graduates who applied for and subsequently accepted positions with independent schools.

Because of the recent budget cuts, school systems have suffered severe cutbacks in expenditures in all areas including teacher hiring and salary increases. But positions do exist, especially in math and computer sciences. Many teachers retire, leave the profession, or find administrative positions, creating thousands of openings each year. Willingness to relocate increases their chances of finding a position.

In 1978 a law was passed mandating special education for all handicapped children. The number of special education teachers rose more than 30 percent between 1970 and 1980, to 187,900. The Department of Education is still predicting a shortage of special ed teachers as the population of children needing special education continues to grow. Job supply is not the only incentive for entering this area; generally, special ed teachers are paid anywhere from $500 to $2000 more per year than other teachers.

Many parents are turning to church-affiliated institutions for the education of their children. Although salaries are almost always lower, job prospects in this area will grow.

New opportunities also exist in the areas of continuing education and preschool education. Adult education courses on virtually every subject imaginable are taught all over the country at local libraries and community centers. The need for nursery schools, some operated by teachers from their own homes, is growing as more and more mothers of young children work full- or part-time.

Geographic Job Index

The majority of jobs are found in suburban school systems and city schools; fewer positions are available in rural and remote regions. New York, California, Texas, Pennsylvania, Michigan, and Illinois have the greatest teacher populations and the greatest number of new openings for teachers. Since the southwestern and mountain states are growing considerably in population and school enrollments are on the rise, the need for teachers in those areas is growing at a faster rate than anywhere else in the country.

Who the Employers Are

PUBLIC SCHOOLS

Secondary positions: 925,000
Elementary positions: 1,175,000

PRIVATE SCHOOLS

Secondary positions: 93,000
Elementary positions: 184,000

California leads the country in the number of private schools with 2444. Of these, 1574 are under the auspices of a religious organization. New York, with 1923, comes in second; 1504 of these schools are church-affiliated.

How to Break into the Field

Teacher certification requirements vary according to state and are always handled by the state's department of education. The best way to find out how to be certified in a given state is to seek advice from the education department of your college. Many schools of education are members of the National Council of Accreditation of Teacher Education, and graduates of these schools are most likely to be certifiable in every state. Certain education requirements are necessary for teaching in public schools; for teaching in public or most private high schools, you are also required to have majored in the subject in which you wish to teach. Private elementary and high schools usually do not require either certification or education courses.

College placement offices provide the most information and the best service in the quest for a teaching position. Local school systems keep them informed of openings, and more distant job opportunities can be found on their bulletin boards as well. Information can also be found in the classified sections of local newspapers.

An interesting cover letter and résumé addressed to a principal will usually produce a response or an application form. Visiting the community in which you want to find a job can produce contacts and word of mouth recommendations.

Personal recommendations are always a good way to secure a job, particularly in an independent school. Application to an independent school is made to the headmaster through a letter of introduction, and a résumé that should include any extracurricular activities that would make you a more valuable staff member. The best time to apply is in the fall before the year in which you wish to be employed. Hiring decisions are usually made in March or April.

To save time and gather information about out-of-town schools, it can be useful to contact national placement organizations.

Among these are:

North American Educational Consultants
P.O. Box 995
Barre, VT 05641
802-479-0157
(specializes in secondary schools here and abroad)

Careers in Education
P.O. Box 455
East Stroudsburg, PA 18301

Independent Education Services
80 Nassau Street
Princeton, NJ 08540
800-257-5102 (toll free) or 609-921-6195
(specializes in placing prospective private school teachers)

Independent Educational Counselors Association
P.O. Box 125
Forest, MA 02644
(specializes in independent schools for the learning disabled)

International Job Opportunities

Opportunities to teach abroad in a variety of subject areas are available to elementary and secondary school teachers through a program sponsored by the United States Information Agency. An applicant must have at least a bachelor's degree, be a United States citizen, and have three years of successful full-time teaching experience, preferably in the subject and at the level for which an application is made. Information and application materials may be obtained from:

Teacher Exchange Branch
United States Information Agency
301 Fourth Street, S.W.
Washington, DC 20547

Opportunities to teach abroad aren't limited to those with three years of teaching experience. For example, speaking Russian can lead you to be sponsored by the American Field Service to participate in an exchange program with the Soviet Union. The Peace Corps, the National Education Association, and UNESCO all offer opportunities for teachers abroad. The most comprehensive brochure on the subject, *Study and Teaching Opportunities Abroad* by Pat Kern McIntyre, can be obtained from the U.S. Department of Education, Washington, DC 20402.

TEACHING

Qualifications

Personal: A genuine desire to work with and care for young people. Ability to lead a group. Strong character. Stamina. Creativity. Well organized.

Professional: College degree. For public schools, certification as well. High school teachers are usually required to have majored in the subject they choose to teach. For elementary school teaching you need a broad range of knowledge and interests, including some instinct for children and how they develop.

Career Paths

LEVEL	JOB TITLE	EXPERIENCE NEEDED
Entry	Teacher	College degree; certification as required
1	Teacher (with master's)	Master's degree in education or in subject area
3	Department Head (high school)	7-10 years

Job Responsibilities

Entry Level

THE BASICS: Presenting subject matter. Developing lesson plans. Preparing and giving examinations. Arranging class and individual projects that contribute to the learning process. Attending parent conferences, field trips, and faculty meetings. In junior and senior high schools, homeroom guidance, study hall supervision.

MORE CHALLENGING DUTIES: Club leadership. Sports coach or leading support for sports activities. Directing activities in which the entire school participates, such as assemblies or fund raisers.

Moving Up

Opportunities for advancement exist in the field of education, especially for those with energy, ideas, and the ability to communicate with both adults and children. Administrators, principals, and superintendents can earn up to $45,000 per year and have a major influence on the communities they serve. To move into administrative or supervisory positions, you must have one year of graduate education, several years of classroom experience, and sometimes a special certificate, depending on the state.

The concept of master teacher is a new one, but school systems in Texas are already awarding teachers who achieve this level—by virtue of experience and effectiveness—with greater responsibility, status and a significant increase in pay. High school teachers have the opportunity to become department heads.

Good and creative teachers with some years of experience are in an excellent position to become educational consultants either as editors of textbooks, directors of special programs, or within the school system as curriculum developers. Especially in the areas of math and the sciences, experienced teachers are being pulled from the classroom to teach other teachers.

To move up in the field of education, you have to have the ability to deal with all kinds of people in all kinds of sensitive situations.

You must have a dedication to the job that continues long after school's over. And you must show a willingness to continue your own education, gaining a master's degree or even a doctoral degree in education or in your subject area.

Teaching can also be a springboard into other professions. Businesses have long known that the experience one gets as a teacher is excellent training for executive positions in marketing, public relations, and advertising. The analytical skills that teachers develop in the classroom, as well as the ability to deal with many different people at many different levels, cannot be taught in a business school. These skills that teachers use day in and day out can be effectively transferred to the business world.

ADDITIONAL INFORMATION

Salaries

Teachers progress in salary as they gain experience. Salaries vary widely from state to state. Starting annual salaries can range from $10,000 to $16,000, but generally higher salaries are to be found in the suburban areas. According to the National Educational Association, for secondary and elementary teachers, in 1982-83, the state with the highest average annual salary was Alaska at $33,953. Washington, DC, came in second with an average salary of $26,045. The lowest paying states were Mississippi, with $14,285; Arkansas, with $15,176; and Vermont, with $15,338.

The salary of an independent secondary school teacher is not commensurate with that of a public school teacher, although there are fringe benefits that can often compensate for the difference in pay. At boarding schools, teachers can expect to receive free room and board or rent-reduced housing on or near campus. Travel expenses and smaller workloads also help to compensate for smaller salaries.

Working Conditions

Hours: Most teachers spend between six and seven hours a day with 15 to 30 children, but that is far from the end of the day. Experienced teachers can often get by with a quick review of their old lesson plans, but new teachers should anticipate an extra two or three hours a day for preparation and correction. Some of the work can be done during the summer vacation and the three or four weeks of holiday during the year.

Environment: This can range from the rolling hills of a rural boarding school to the bleak insides of an inner-city school. Teachers can have access to tennis courts, swimming pools, even a stable full of horses, or they may have to content themselves, for recreation, with the smoke-filled faculty room.

The classroom environment is generally what you make it. Elementary teachers can plaster their walls with children's art, waxed leaves in fall, cutouts of flowers in spring. In secondary schools, decoration can be anything from a chart of chemical elements to a poster of the rock star of the moment.

Workstyle: Most classrooms consist of a blackboard, a big desk, and 20 or 30 smaller ones facing front. Yet each teacher has the choice to make each class either student-centered or teacher-centered. Some teachers prefer to lecture or read to their students; other promote student discussion to various degrees. History teachers have discovered that role-playing and mini-dramas can give life to an epoch. English classes can concentrate on grammar, literature, or writing. With the availability of computers, students are less likely to tune out of math class because of the possibilities for direct interaction and feedback. The art room can offer the freest environment. Many teachers turn on music while students paint or sculpt, and students chat among themselves or with the teacher as they work. The major environmental factor in any class will always be the moods and attitudes of the students, and this is where the good teacher becomes the chief architect of his or her surroundings.

Travel: If travel is your end, teaching abroad can be your means. Class trips and outings are also available to the enterprising teacher. Schools will often pay the expenses of a teacher attending a conference, chaperoning a team to an out-of-town match, or accompanying students to recreational activities.

Extracurricular Activities/Work Experience

Volunteer—Big Brother/Sister program, tutoring, sports, summer camps, teen counseling, child care centers for retarded or culturally disadvantaged children

Athletics—sports (participation can lead to coaching positions in secondary schools)

School—cheerleading, debate society, literary clubs, student newspapers, yearbook publications, student government, drama club, glee club, art club, alumni/admissions administrative work

Internships

Aside from the student teaching that accompanies college or graduate certification and degree programs, there are few opportunities for teaching internships, except at a limited number of independent schools. They offer the opportunity to get experience in teaching without taking on the responsibility of a full-time teacher. Under the tutelage of a head teacher, the intern learns the ins and outs of the profession. Both school and intern benefit from such a program and the intern is often paid a nominal salary. Contact individual independent schools to see if they have a program.

Recommended Reading

BOOKS

Don't Smile Until Christmas: Accounts of the First Year of Teaching, Kevin Ryan, ed. University of Chicago Press: 1970

The Teacher Rebellion by David Selden, Howard University Press: 1970

Teaching School: Points Picked Up by Eric Johnson, Walker & Company: 1979

PERIODICALS

Academic Journal: The Educator's Employment Magazine (biweekly), Box 392, Newton, CT 06470

American Education (ten times a year), U.S. Department of Education, 400 Maryland Avenue, S.W., Washington, DC 20202

Arithmetic Teacher/Mathematics Teacher (ten times a year), 11906 Association Drive, Reston, VA 22091

The Association for School, College and University (ASCUS) Staffing Annual: A Job Search Handbook for Educators (annual), Box 411, Madison, WI 53711

Chronicle of Higher Education (weekly), 1333 New Hampshire Avenue, N.W., Washington, DC 20036

Harvard Educational Review (quarterly), Graduate School of Education, Harvard University, 13 Appian Way, Cambridge, MA 02138

Today's Education (quarterly), National Education Association, 1201 Sixteenth Street, N.W., Washington, DC 20036

Professional Associations

American Federation of Teachers
11 Dupont Circle, N.W.
Washington, DC 20036

Association for School, College and University Staffing
ASCUS Office
Box 411
Madison, WI 53711

National Education Association
1201 Sixteenth Street, N.W.
Washington, DC 20036

INTERVIEWS

Margaret Thompson, Age 39
Secondary School Teacher
Needham High School and Newman Middle School, Needham, MA

Although the competition for English teaching positions is very fierce now, in five or ten years there should be a real market. If you're lucky enough to find a position right now, though, it can be the most rewarding experience of your life.

There's autonomy. You're your own boss. Once you're in that classroom, the door is shut. You can be amazingly creative. Every single day is a new challenge. And you get to show off a lot. Probably more than any other subject, teaching English calls on you to perform.

Teaching English is like conducting an orchestra. You're in charge, but the students have to play their own instruments. The more they play their instruments, the happier they are. And when they can hear those instruments being played together in an orchestra it gives them a big thrill.

For example, sixth and seventh graders are being introduced to literature for the first time in their lives; you teach them about the components of a story—the climax, the development, the resolution; then they read the story and for the first time have a sense of recognition; they're reading about characters who are experiencing some of the same conflicts they are. They listen to each other's interpretations and all of a sudden they don't feel alone anymore.

I think literature is one of the most subtle ways of affecting people's lives. You have to know how to choose the literature that will be the catalyst to self-understanding and give students the structural tools to explore their own lives.

What kind of person would really have fun teaching? A caring person. One who enjoys stroking and being stroked. I've been teaching for 13 years now. I'm making about maximum salary, $26,000 a year. But the feeling of loving more than balances the salary. I'll never stop teaching. It's a joy.

Laura Daigen, Age 29
Fourth-Grade Teacher
New York, NY

I started out teaching Spanish in a high school, but I decided there was a lot more good to be done as a bilingual elementary teacher. I was somewhat disillusioned with the politics of the school where I worked. Teachers who had been there longer made sure that they had no problem students in their classes and that kids with low test scores were taught by the rookies. The Spanish language textbooks were poor and antiquated in their absence of girls and women.

When you're working in a public school in the inner city, the needs of your kids are infinite. There's very little support from the administration or cohesiveness among the faculty. You're alone with kids who have more emotional needs than you can deal with. There is no one to help you help them.

Even under the best of conditions, the hours are long. Sometimes I'm there until six or seven and I'm not the last one to leave. I'm making plans for new curriculum, I'm marking papers, I'm cleaning up the room. You're never finished when you're a teacher: you dream it, you go to sleep thinking about it, and you wake up thinking about it. You're teaching eleven pieces of curriculum and you have to coordinate them and give enough time to each one. It was easier teaching Spanish in a high school, because I was teaching one subject at three different levels and the students had the responsibility of absorbing what you gave them. But when you're teaching elementary school and the kid isn't learning, it's your fault.

If someone were trying to decide whether or not to go into teaching, the first question I would ask him or her is: Do you like kids? Are you ready to take on the responsibility of little human beings and their emotional needs? There is tremendous satisfaction in watching children grow, seeing them move out of themselves and being able to give; recognizing their right to receive fair treatment knowing they can effect change if they see an injustice being done. It feels great to have a kid say, "I like math this year," or "I don't have to try to read these books, I can just read them," or to see kids take charge of their own lives and take pride in what they've done on their own.

I think what makes a good teacher is the sincerity of his or her commitment—whatever it is. It can be to help children love reading or to help them see themselves as important pieces of society or to help them realize the value of their own ethnicity. It has to be more than a vague "I love kids"—but you have to love kids, too.

No matter what I end up doing with my life, I'll always be able to look back on these five or six years and say those were years that I spent doing what I really wanted to do. Perhaps I haven't been well-compensated economically, but the job is rewarding. I will always be able to say that I did something that was meaningful, something that helped others.

HUMAN SERVICES

A constellation of diverse occupations grouped under the general heading of human services presents a wide choice for those graduates who have a special feeling for working with people. Patience, sincere interest in others, a caring attitude, and a real desire to help the less fortunate are necessary conditions for these jobs—but they are not sufficient ones. A constructive tough-mindedness is equally imperative. Along with the satisfaction of seeing tangible results and of being able to effect positive changes in the lives of those in trouble come frustrations of all sorts: the daily encounter with personal tragedies; the discouraging effort to make even a small dent in seemingly intractable social problems. But if you are equipped to maintain the necessary precarious balance, a career in one of the helping professions, as they are often called, may well be for you.

Your college studies have given you some understanding of the diversity of human interaction and the consequences of an individual's inability to function. But undergraduate training only lays the groundwork for a career in human services. Advanced degrees, such as a master's in social work or occupational therapy, or a doctorate or credentials for certain specialties, such as counseling alcoholics, are not only required for advancement, but are needed for many entry-level jobs. Although there are employers who will hire job candidates with only a bachelor's degree, your career prospects will become severely limited if you do not augment your education and training.

The types of jobs you might be offered if you have no advanced degree vary. Some entry-level jobs can be very challenging; others are of the paraprofessional variety, and are low paying and do not always involve you in highly challenging work.

Jobs may be found in the following areas of human services:

- **Counseling**
- **Psychology Paraprofessionals**
- **Administration**
- **Advocacy**
- **Research**
- **Community Relations**
- **Program Development**

These positions are available in a wide variety of institutions and agencies. There are social service agencies in the federal, state, and local governments, and national, state, and local private nonprofit organizations as well. Coupled with private and public institutions and health care facilities, these represent a sizable job bank. However, since much of the funding for human services, both public and private, depends on the federal government, the number of jobs available and the salaries they offer vary with the political climate. At the present time there is relatively little money being invested in these services, and many institutions have been forced to cut back on their programs.

Job Outlook

Job Openings Will Grow: More slowly than average

Competition for Jobs: Keen
Graduates should realize that the human services are among the most competitive of all professions. Dedication, a solid record of academic achievement, and self-confidence are important attributes in job seekers.

New Job Opportunities: Demographic projections indicate that our population will have a higher percentage of elderly people in the decades to come. This change will produce an increased demand for geriatric care and counseling and other services for the elderly. Jobs will also be opening up in alcohol and substance abuse programs. The profession is moving away from its traditional dependence on large institutions; new jobs are going to be in small, nonconventional facilities such as halfway houses and hospices.

Many of the most difficult to fill jobs in human services require foreign language abilities. If you can converse easily in Spanish or (although less frequently required) some other language, you find more jobs open to you.

Geographic Job Index

There are jobs in government agencies and private organizations throughout the country. Many agencies and services operate in cities, but jobs are not limited to urban areas. The offices that administer many federal agencies are situated in or near Washington, DC, although the people who actually provide the services are located in every state. Because of the difficulty of finding entry-level positions, a willingness to relocate will provide you with more options.

Who the Employers Are

NATIONAL NONPROFIT ORGANIZATIONS employ people in all functional areas. In branches throughout the country, organizations such as the YMCA or the Boys' Clubs of America hire counselors, advocates, and program development staffs. These local branches also have administrative and community relations posts. Naturally there is a wider selection of administrative, research, and program development positions at national headquarters.

Most nonprofit agencies are organized around a specific social issue. For example, Goodwill Industries of America is concerned with helping the physically disabled; Planned Parenthood deals with family planning and women's reproductive freedom. Examine your own interests and beliefs and try to choose an agency whose work is important to you. You will be more effective in, and get more satisfaction from, a job you believe in.

THE FEDERAL GOVERNMENT provides most social services through the Department of Health and Human Services. Its agencies, such as the Administration on Aging, the Office of Child Development, and the Office for Handicapped Individuals, address specific social issues. The Department of Justice and the Veterans' Administration are also good sources of jobs for recent graduates. Depending on the department or agency, a wide variety of positions is available in counseling, program development, administration, and research. The major drawback to federal jobs is their sensitivity to the political climate. A change of administration can affect personnel, hiring, funding, and the fundamental goals of an agency.

STATE AND LOCAL GOVERNMENTS provide numerous jobs in all functional areas.

COMMUNITY MENTAL HEALTH FACILITIES AND HOSPITALS hire those with a B.A. degree as mental health paraprofessionals whose principal job is to assist psychologists. Substantive mental health care is provided by professional psychologists with advanced degrees.

How to Break into the Field

Practical experience is the key. A job in human services stresses interpersonal relationships and commitment, and any experience you have working with people is a plus. Look into volunteer work: you might try peer counseling at a college drop-in center, or helping out at an event such as the Special Olympics for handicapped people. Paid experience carries even more weight than volunteer work. A paid part-time or summer job in human services can help enormously in making contacts and in making a good impression on an interviewer.

Although a good résumé and cover letter may win you an interview, your performance at the interview will be the most important factor in whether you are hired. The interviewer will be assessing your interpersonal skills. Developing a rapport and confidently communicating your abilities and experience are vital skills.

To get an entry-level position with the federal government you should start at a Federal Job Information Center, which is listed under United States Government in the telephone book. These centers provide specific information on what jobs are available, which forms you must file, and whether a civil service examination is required.

For information on state employment, contact the state personnel department; for local work, the county or city personnel office.

International Job Opportunities

Although you will not be able to find a job in human services abroad, a number of options are open to you if you want to gain insights into the needs of people in other nations. The American Friends Service Committee, various church-affiliated organizations, and the Peace Corps are among the organizations that send volunteers abroad. Such programs are usually competitive—the Peace Corps is especially selective—but they take recent graduates. Such positions test your endurance, your commitment, and your ability to serve the needs of others.

COUNSELING

A counseling position allows the most direct contact with those you are trying to help. Counselors who work in crisis intervention, rehabilitation, guidance, or within a direct care facility for the mentally retarded or the physically disabled often need only a B.A. degree and some experience in counseling. They may work with clients face-to-face or via a phone-in hotline. These jobs are oriented toward solving urgent, immediate problems rather than deep psychological disabilities. They combine sympathy and understanding with practical resources that facilitate day-to-day living for those faced with a variety of problems—physical abuse, drug or alcohol addiction, or unemployment, to name a few.

Counseling work provides the emotional, intellectual and psychological benefits that result from changing people's lives for the better. Most counselors find it particularly rewarding to work with those to whom they are naturally drawn. Some prefer working with emotionally disturbed children; others find satisfaction in helping the elderly. Knowing your own predilections can make a big difference in how well you do your job and the amount of satisfaction you derive from it.

A related profession is guidance counseling, which involves working with students in schools. State certification is required; qualifications vary, but they may include advanced training, certification to teach, and, in some states, teaching experience. In addition to offering vocational advice, guidance counselors help students handle academic, social, and behavioral problems.

Qualifications:

Personal: A desire to help people on a one-to-one basis. The ability to listen to and empathize with a client. Capacity for working with other counselors.

Professional: A knowledge of social issues and problems. Writing and basic research skills. Knowledge of the resources available to counselors.

Job Responsibilities

Entry Level

THE BASICS: Talking to clients in person or on a telephone hotline. Keeping records of counseling sessions. Maintaining a referral file. Clerical duties.

MORE CHALLENGING DUTIES: Contacting and dealing with other service agencies. Handling difficult client cases. Attending staff meetings and seminars. Preparing reports, charts, and statistical records.

Moving Up

For many people who work as counselors, moving up means taking an administrative or supervisory position. Such a position would usually entail overseeing and organizing a staff of counselors.

To progress beyond that level, a counselor needs an advanced degree. Many people who have worked as counselors and administrators often go into program development and community relations. Because these functional areas are all people-oriented jobs, professionals often move among them.

PSYCHOLOGY PARAPROFESSIONAL

Although you may land a job in counseling with only a bachelor's degree, you will probably find that you are best suited to jobs that fall under such titles as mental health assistant, technician, or aide. These paraprofessional positions are usually found in institutional settings such as state hospitals, community mental health centers, facilities for the mentally retarded, or senior citizens centers. Psychology paraprofessionals work under the supervision of a professional psychologist or social worker and usually perform such duties as screening and evaluating new patients, directing patient contact activities, engaging in advocacy of patient needs, and assisting in community consultation. Or you may be assigned to a hotline, talking on the telephone to battered women, possible suicides, or victims of rape or child abuse.

Mental health paraprofessional work is low paying, generally does not carry much status, and often includes a great deal of drudge work. Nevertheless, such jobs are a source of experience and give you an opportunity to discover whether you have the desire and temperament to become a professional psychologist or social worker.

ADMINISTRATION

Administrative work requires a good sense of organization. You handle the endless details that keep a service operating smoothly. Responsibilities include everything from overseeing a staff to ordering office supplies. Administrative jobs involve little contact with the people for whom a service exists. However, because you deal with the people who work directly with the clients, you still need to be highly sensitive to the needs of others. Supportive administrators are the first line of defense in a field in which professionals often suffer emotional and physical burnout.

In many health care facilities, you need a master's degree in health care administration, but some government and nonprofit organizations do offer some administrative positions that do not require a master's degree. However, these entry-level jobs may not always involve you in highly challenging work. The most interesting jobs in human services administration often go to people with experience in counseling, advocacy, or some other area of the profession.

Qualifications

Personal: A strong sense of organization. The ability to remain calm under pressure. The skills to supervise others with tact and understanding. Sound judgment. A sense of fairness.

Professional: Typing. Management skills. Financial skills, such as basic accounting. An understanding of the type of service you will help administer.

Job Responsibilities

Entry Level

THE BASICS: Answering phones. Typing. Filing. Filling out forms and writing reports. Assisting higher-level administration.

MORE CHALLENGING DUTIES: Organizing grant proposals. Dealing with other service agencies. Offering support and guidance to front-line staff members.

Moving Up

Administrators must be keenly aware of changes, trends, and developments within the industry. Because human services facilities often have small administrative staffs, you may have to change employers in order to move into higher-level jobs.

ADVOCACY

As an advocate it is your job to bring people in need together with existing services that might help them. Advocates might guide an ex-convict back into community life, get welfare services for poor people, or find jobs for the mentally or physically disabled, or for reformed alcoholics or drug abusers. You act as a go-between, connecting people with employers, counseling services, medical services, and so on.

Advocacy requires a great deal of tact, a sense of justice, and a desire to see people treated fairly. You must competently handle a wide variety of cases—some simple, some complex—while maintaining good relationships with your contacts and support services. It takes persistence, patience, and determination—and the frustrations are many. You must learn not to feel personally responsible when, despite your hard work, results on a case are less than you had hoped for. The paperwork is voluminous and never-ending. But the results, when you achieve them, are tangible and rewarding.

Advocates work for both private and government-sponsored agencies. Like counselors, advocates may follow any number of career paths, often moving into other human services jobs.

The most recognizable advocates in the community are parole and probation officers. They help reintegrate ex-convicts into society by finding them jobs, getting them drug or alcohol counseling when needed, locating houses, and mediating contacts with other agencies. Parole and probation officers are hired by federal, state, or local governments; for many positions, you will be required to pass an exam. There will be an initial training period—in a classroom, on the job, or some combination of the two. Because these jobs are part and parcel of the bureaucracy, moving up depends as often on seniority (and sometimes even political considerations) as it does on skill.

RESEARCH

Research work offers the least amount of contact with the people who need the human services. Nevertheless, it is the foundation upon which the helping professions are built. It ensures that existing programs are working successfully and determines where new programs are needed.

Research requires strong quantitative skills and a gift for statistical analysis. It is definitely not a job for anyone with a fear of math. You also need good writing skills because once your research is completed, you will be asked to analyze and report on the results and, at higher levels, write proposals for new programs or improvements in existing ones.

The majority of research positions are found in the federal government, particularly in the Department of Health and Human Services and the National Institute of Education (a division of the

Department of Education). Innovative psychological investigations have been done by the Office of Naval Research and other federal agencies. Today, however, hiring freezes have drastically cut the number of job openings.

The future of human services research is closely related to computer technology. Research now relies heavily on the abilities of the computer to correlate facts and figures. The profession is moving toward what is known as "hard" research, that is, research that places a strong emphasis on numerical findings.

The entry-level position in research is the journeyman or woman, open to those with a college degree, some knowledge of the research subject, and a strong background in statistics and methods of testing. At this level you will compile and sort data; check facts, figures, and sources; and enter data into a data base. More challenging duties may include reading research proposals and briefings in order to contribute to brainstorming meetings and research presentations. However, to progress in any tangible way in this area you will need an advanced degree in a specialized area.

COMMUNITY RELATIONS

For any human service to have value, the people who most need it must know about it and have access to it. Community relations workers fill this vital need. By keeping lines of communication open between service organizations and the community, they make the public aware of offered services, find out the community's opinion of existing programs, and determine what the public thinks is needed for the future.

The community relations staff work closely with the organization's administration in order to ensure that services are reaching those who need them. They also see that as wide an audience as possible knows about the organization's work, so a working knowledge of public relations and publicity is a plus.

It is rare to find an entry-level position in community relations. Rather, it is an area to which people come after serving in counseling, advocacy, or administrative positions. Because much of the work involves meeting with community groups, a solid background knowledge of community problems and needs is essential. You must also be a good organizer and have the ability to bring people and ideas together.

PROGRAM DEVELOPMENT

Social service agencies cannot address the needs of their clients without carefully- and well-designed programs. This work requires creative, innovative, and farsighted people who are able to examine all aspects of a problem and devise a workable solution. Like community relations, the area of program development is not for entry-level personnel, but one you enter with experience and an advanced degree.

Program development is for team players: everyone involved with a project shares ideas and information. No one person can be expected to see all sides of a problem, so program designers must be open to suggestions, and receptive to contributions from researchers, administrators, and community relations staff. Ultimately, though, it is up to those in program development to pull all the available information together and come up with a plan of action.

Unless you communicate well, your brainchild hasn't a chance to become the program you imagined it to be. You must be able to put your ideas in writing effectively. To move from an ideal to a completed program you must be flexible and willing to revise, rework, and rewrite a proposal many times.

A good deal of reading is required to keep up with social trends, current research, and innovations in service programs. Maintaining contacts with agencies and organizations other than your own is also important. Most of all, however, you must never lose sight of your clients' needs if your work is to serve them well.

ADDITIONAL INFORMATION

Salaries

Salaries in the human services are notoriously low, especially when you consider the amount of advanced training required for many positions. Entry-level salaries in social service and mental health facilities fall between $10,000 and $17,000 per year; the salaries available to graduates without training beyond the bachelor's degree fall into the lower end of this range. Government employees, such as probation officers, earn slightly better pay.

If you do advance to positions of responsibility without getting further training, you cannot expect to earn more than $20,000 per year. The highest salaries in the field go to people with advanced degrees and a field of specialization. An experienced research development specialist, for example, may earn $35,000 per year.

Working Conditions

Hours: Working days are long in the human services. Your hours will be determined by the programs you are involved in and the types of people you serve. The most regular schedules (that is, a basic five-day work week) belong to administrative personnel and researchers. But in any of the helping professions, meetings, paperwork, and the pressures created by chronic understaffing will often require you to work evenings and weekends. You must also keep up with current developments in your field through outside reading. The burdens of the long work week fall most heavily on counselors—some feel they never leave work, but carry it at all times.

Environment: Office space is usually cramped and the office appearance is best described as functional. At the entry level your chances of having a private office are slim, but experienced people will normally have their own offices. Counselors and advocates are provided with quiet, comfortable, private areas to meet with their clients.

Workstyle: Counselors and advocates spend much of their time with clients, doing follow-up paperwork and meeting with other staff members to share experiences and discuss cases. Administrators are often at their desks and participate in frequent meetings. Although much of a researcher's day is spent in solitary work—going over printouts, writing reports, and so forth—project and strategy development are group efforts.

Travel: Travel is not usually a part of a job in the human services, but senior personnel and, less frequently, junior people may travel to conferences and conventions.

Extracurricular Activities/Work Experience

Volunteer work, summer, or part-time jobs at: college counseling services; hospitals, mental health centers, or nursing homes; local branches of national nonprofit organizations; hotlines for suicide, rape, child abuse, battered women, or other problems; church-affiliated charity organizations.

Membership in a service fraternity or sorority: Alpha Phi Alpha (fraternity), Alpha Kappa Alpha (sorority), Alpha Phi Omega (open to men and women).

Internships

Many internship opportunities exist in the human service professions. Community and social service facilities often need assistance. Because these facilities normally have limited financial resources, paid internships are difficult to find, but many programs offer academic credit. Potential sponsors are selective when choosing interns. You must demonstrate a sincere interest in the facility's services and a willingness to learn. If you are interested in working with children, you might also consider an internship at a day care center or a similar facility.

Recommended Reading

BOOKS

Directory of Agencies: U.S. Voluntary, International Voluntary, Intergovernmental, National Association of Social Workers: 1980

Employment and Unemployment in Social Work: A Study of N.A.S.W. Members by David A. Hardcastle and Arthur J. Katz, National Association of Social Workers: 1979

Helping Others by Anthony D'Augelli, et al., Brooks-Cole: 1980

National Directory of Mental Health, John Wiley and Sons: 1980

National Directory of Private Social Agencies, Croner Publications: 1983

New Careers and Roles in the Helping Professions by Robert J. Wicks, C.C. Thomas: 1979

The Social Worker Grid by Robert R. Blake, C.C. Thomas: 1979

PERIODICALS

Child Development (quarterly), University of Chicago Press, Journals Division, 5801 Ellis Avenue, Chicago, IL 60637

Child Welfare (monthly), Child Welfare League of America, 67 Irving Place, New York, NY 10003

Community Mental Health Journal (quarterly), 72 Fifth Avenue, New York, NY 10001

Corrections Magazine (bimonthly), Criminal Justice Publications, 116 West 32nd Street, New York, NY 10001

Crime and Delinquency (quarterly), National Council on Crime and Delinquency, 411 Hackensack Avenue, Hackensack, NJ 07601

Family Relations (quarterly), National Council on Family Relations, 1219 University Avenue, S.E., Minneapolis, MN 55414

The Gerontologist (bimonthly), Gerontological Society, 1835 K Street, N.W., Washington, DC 20006

Journal of Counseling Psychology (bimonthly), American Psychological Association, 1200 17th Street, N.W., Washington, DC 20036

Journal of Social Psychology (quarterly), Journal Press, 2 Commercial Street, Provincetown, MA 02657

Psychology Today (monthly), 1 Park Avenue, New York, NY 10016

Professional Associations

American Association of Mental Health Professionals in Corrections
c/o Veterans Administration Mental Health Center
2615 East Clinton
Fresno, CA 93703

American Family Therapy Association
2550 M Street, N.W.
Suite 275
Washington, DC 20037

American Mental Health Counselor Association
1215 Norman Hall
University of Florida
Gainesville, FL 32611

Mental Health Association
1800 North Kent Street
Rosslyn, VA 22209

National Alliance for the Mentally Ill
1234 Massachusetts Avenue, N.W.
Washington, DC 20005

National Institute of Mental Health
Department of Health and Human Services
Rockville, MD 20857

INTERVIEWS

Elizabeth Tower, Age 26
Crisis Intervention Counselor
Victims Services, New York, NY

I began crisis intervention counseling four years ago, right after I graduated from college. I have seen and heard a lot from people who feel very desperate. They are at a point in their lives where they need immediate help. For many people who call on the hotline, we are their last chance. I get an incredible amount of satisfaction from helping people to cope and, in some cases, to survive.

A lot of the calls on the hotline are from battered women. It is a tremendous social problem. Many women are too embarrassed or too scared to confide in friends or relatives. I hear heartbreaking stories, but helping a woman get out of a terrible situation makes it all worthwhile. We literally save people's lives.

You need to have a commitment to working with people. I believe that the work I do is solving social problems on a grass-roots level. I can't change all the problems in our society, but I can help one person at a time, and I think that is a part of positive social change. Of course, you don't always feel totally positive about your work. It can be very emotionally draining when you become involved in other people's problems. Fortunately, counseling is a group effort: I get an enormous amount of support from the people I work with. We have all learned that you have to deal with your own frustration and limitations.

Debbie Clark, Age 28
Residence Manager
Yorkville Residence for Mentally Retarded Adults, New York, NY

My first job in human services was working with emotionally disturbed deaf and hearing-impaired adolescents as a live-in counselor. That had to be the most exhausting job on earth. If one of the kids started acting up in the middle of the night, you couldn't just roll over and go back to sleep—you had to respond to the situation. I think that is really what human services is about—responding to a need where and when it comes up.

I majored in psychology in college and then went straight on for a master's in guidance and counseling. With that degree completed, I started working with the disturbed adolescents. I was promoted from direct care worker to supervisor. During my third year at that residence, I started a master's in social work, but only completed one year of study. I first worked with mentally retarded adults when I moved to another agency as an assistant manager of a group home, and changed jobs yet again when I came into my present position.

My present job is managing a residence for mentally retarded adults. Homes like these allow mentally retarded people to leave institutional settings and try to live more normal lives. Basically my job is to take care of everything—from scheduling the staff to ordering paper towels. I keep things running smoothly and handle any emergencies that come up. Even though my current job is not a live-in position, it certainly is a 24-hour-a-day job. I'm always available in case of an emergency.

You're probably wondering why on earth I do this. Well, the bottom line is that I truly care about these people. They have been abused and mistreated for most of their lives, and you've got to be really determined when you start fighting for people who can't fight for themselves. I am proud of the house I run; we create a caring space for people who have lived under inhuman conditions and you can see them respond to it. I don't like the long hours, but I love the way I feel about my job and myself.

MARKET RESEARCH

In ancient times, people flocked to star-gazers and oracles to ask about the future. Today predictions are made by market researchers, who try to foresee if a particular group—consumers, businesspeople, voters—will believe in a product, a business decision, a candidate, or an idea. Rather than consulting the stars or relying on their instincts, market researchers base their predictions on research. They spend days, weeks, months, and even years sampling opinions, tastes, and reactions.

Many variables besides quality account for success or failure in the marketplace—changing tastes and trends, public perceptions (and misconceptions), subliminal messages. Before a new product appears in the stores, before an old favorite gets new packaging, even before a product is discontinued, market research is conducted and its conclusions incorporated into business strategies and advertising campaigns.

Food processors and manufacturers of cosmetics and consumer goods need to know who will buy a certain product and why, what kind of packaging is most enticing and appropriate, how much consumers are willing to pay, and how frequently consumers will use the product. To find the answers, new products are tested against established ones, facsimiles of the product are test-marketed, and surveys of potential consumers are made. The results may confirm a company's conviction that a sufficient market for a given product exists or that it is the right time to introduce such a product. Market researchers often suggest pricing and marketing strategies based on consumer responses.

Research may be concerned with something other than a consumer product. Current issues, the ramifications of business decisions, and even political campaigns are studied through market research. Regardless of the subject, all research follows a similar pattern—the problem is defined, a research strategy is developed, information is collected and analyzed, and the results are interpreted and presented to the users. Information may be gleaned from phone interviews, on-the-scene impromptu interviews with a target group (e.g., moviegoers, shoppers), written surveys or focus groups, the carefully selected people who fit the demographics of the client's intended market.

Two different types of work go into market research: data collection and information analysis. Data collection is the more detailed. It involves tallying questionnaires, conducting phone interviews, and assembling relevant printed information. Much of the research is either quantitative or qualitative. Quantitative research tends to produce numbers-oriented studies; qualitative reports feature more subjective information, such as opinion sampling. Information analysis is more sophisticated work; it involves interpreting the results of the research and writing up conclusions in a report or presentation for the client. There is also tedious number-crunching work, which is given to the least experienced people. But computers are eliminating the drudgery of such work and, best of all, drastically reducing the amount of time needed to do complicated cross-tabulations.

Some companies do both information collection and analysis, but market research firms often rely on tabulation services and field services to perform the time-consuming tasks that precede analysis. Tabulation services specialize in collecting data of any sort, usually through surveys and questionnaires supplied by the research company. They do not analyze the data, they simply collect it. Field services perform a more personalized aspect of the same task. They specialize in interviews that take many forms: with groups, with individuals, by phone, or in shopping centers. These companies may tabulate the results for their clients.

Market research is a growing field that is extending its influence into businesses of all kinds and to hospitals, colleges, and other nonprofit organizations that need to know how to manage their own development, who their constituency is or ought to be, and, often most important, how to target potential contributions and successfully solicit donations.

No one specific academic background is required for a job in market research, but you must be able to work effectively and comfortably with numbers and to articulate your ideas clearly and convincingly. Although an undergraduate degree is all you'll need to get an entry-level position, you should be prepared to take some graduate courses if you want to make your career in this field. Although you don't have to be a math major to do quantitative research, you will probably feel more comfortable in that area if you have a strong background in math or statistics. After you gain some experience and demonstrate your ability to grasp quickly what kind of research is necessary in any particular client situation, you should be able to move up into a challenging position.

Job Outlook

Job Openings Will Grow: Faster than average

Competition for Jobs: Keen

New Job Opportunities: Expansion in the industry is taking place in research companies—independent firms that offer research services to clients. As new service industries, such as the newly expanding banking industry and cable television, continue to enter the marketplace, the need for research companies will grow.

Geographic Job Index

New York, NY, and Chicago, IL, are the leading centers of market research, but job opportunities exist across the country, mostly—but not exclusively—in urban areas.

Who the Employers Are

MARKET RESEARCH FIRMS perform complete research studies, although they may use outside tabulation houses and field services for data collection. Once they receive the data, they analyze and report on the data to their clients. They may also initiate their own research projects and then sell the findings to interested companies. Research companies often specialize in a single type of client. As a result, many firms have staffs of fewer than ten people.

CONSUMER GOODS MANUFACTURING FIRMS often have market research departments within their corporate structure. These departments may or may not carry out numerical research, but they design the research projects that need to be done, analyze and interpret the results, and make recommendations based on their conclusions. Usually, only a handful of people are employed in-house, and most of the jobs there go to experienced people.

Major Employers

A.C. Nielsen Company, Northbend, IL
Arbitron Ratings Company, New York, NY
Audits & Surveys, New York, NY
Burke Marketing Services, Cincinnati, OH
IMS International, New York, NY
Market Facts, Chicago, IL
Marketing and Research Counselors, Dallas, TX
NFO Research, Toledo, OH
NPD Group, Port Washington, NY
Sellings Areas-Marketing, Inc., New York, NY

How to Break into the Field

You'll stand a better chance of getting hired in an entry-level job if you have related experience. Field services employ large numbers of high school and undergraduate students in part-time and summer positions, usually as interviewers who call people across the country to ask prepared questions and take responses.

Large firms (those with 40 employees or more) occasionally recruit on campus, but, in general, you will have to investigate openings on your own. Firms are listed in the Yellow Pages under "Marketing Services." Newspaper help-wanted ads normally advertise positions for experienced personnel only. But it's often worthwhile to contact the company that is advertising the job on the chance that the new senior-level person may need an assistant.

The Chemical Marketing Research Association runs a yearly three- or four-day course in July. It's titled Basic Chemical Marketing Research Short Course, but it is a good introduction to the market research process in general. For information, contact the Chemical Marketing Research Association. (Address given at the end of this chapter.)

International Job Opportunities

Market research is done in most Western countries, but international job opportunities are very limited, since most positions are filled by nationals.

RESEARCH ANALYSIS

The entry-level position in research analysis is the junior or associate analyst. You will assist experienced analysts by handling the routine detail work that accompanies all projects. In firms or departments that do field work, you may begin by interviewing or editing and coding—checking to see that all questionnaires are completed and assigning numerical codes to nonnumerical responses so that results can be tabulated. Firms that depend on field services may send new employees to a service for a few weeks so they can get a firsthand understanding of the information-gathering process.

Typically, one analyst is responsible for each project. Besides preparing and presenting the conclusions of a study, this individual must coordinate the efforts of all contributors—one or more junior analysts and field and tabulation personnel. Analysts, especially those in senior or executive positions, may solicit new business and maintain contacts with past clients.

To become a successful market research analyst, you must be able to (1) read a qualitative report and determine what questions need to be asked to get concrete, quantitative answers; (2) produce a logical, coherent picture from the results of a numerical survey or the varied answers of an opinion poll; and (3) communicate effectively, guiding your clients to conclusions that are appropriate to the results of your research, convincing them that your recommendations are well-grounded and credible. Deadline pressure is constant; the entire process of research and analysis often takes no longer than six to ten weeks. You may work on one project at a time or be concerned with several in various stages, and you're sure to have assignments changed suddenly.

Qualifications

Personal: Good judgment. Able to communicate clearly. Personable appearance and manner. Good powers of concentration. Ability to work on a team. Problem-solving mentality.

Professional: Strong writing and communications skills. Math and statistical know-how. Good phone manner. Typing or word processing skills.

Career Paths

LEVEL	JOB TITLE	EXPERIENCE NEEDED
Entry	Coder-editor, junior or associate analyst	College degree
2	Analyst	1-2 years
3	Senior analyst, research manager	4-7 years
4	Market research director	7+ years

Job Responsibilities

Entry Level

THE BASICS: Clerical duties: typing, filing, handling the flow of correspondence. Proofreading questionnaires. Writing cover letters, memos, and progress reports. Organizing completed studies and reports.

MORE CHALLENGING DUTIES: Writing questionnaires, using successful examples. Basic data analysis. Organizing and rearranging tables, charts, and raw data. Writing introductions and reports for coders and interviewers.

Moving Up

The key to success in this competitive business is building an understanding of the research process as quickly as possible. You must demonstrate the ability to study data and apply your conclusions to specific problems. You will not deal directly with the users of the research until you have adequate experience (a year or more). At first, you will meet with brand managers, gathering background information and drafting initial proposals. This work will provide an understanding of user needs. As a researcher handling your own projects, you will respond to these needs through your analyses. A good deal of writing and speaking is involved, and you must be both candid and diplomatic in the way you present results.

ADDITIONAL INFORMATION

Salaries

Each year, the American Marketing Association conducts a salary survey of its members. The average annual salaries for market research personnel nationwide in the 1983 report were:

Analyst	$24,128
Manager or supervisor	$32,945
Director	$41,361
President	$53,483

Working Conditions

Hours: The standard 40-hour week can stretch to 12-hour days and include weekends in times of heavy business. But there are corresponding slack periods. Hours tend to be more regular in the larger research firms and in-house departments.

Environment: Analysts often have their own small offices, and most research firms have at least one larger conference room where analysts will get together to discuss ongoing projects.

Workstyle: The work day is hectic for both entry-level and senior personnel. The junior analyst generally spends each day in the office. Analysts visit clients and potential clients. Research often involves a great deal of phone work.

Travel: Opportunities for national and international travel exist at many research firms. Although field services can provide coverage of virtually any location in the United States, an analyst may occasionally travel to supervise research for an international corporation on market conditions in another part of the globe, or to investigate personally a locale's unique characteristics.

Extracurricular Activities/Work Experience

Business Research Practicum

American Marketing Association—student member

Canvassing/phone interviewing for charities or political campaigns

Campus newspaper—reporting

Internships

There are no formal internship programs in market research, but you can try to set one up on your own by contacting the personnel director in some of the larger companies.

Recommended Reading

PERIODICALS

Careers in Industrial Marketing Research published by The Chemical Marketing Research Association (free)

Careers in Marketing by Neil Hobart, American Marketing Association, Monograph Series #4 (free)

Employment and Career Opportunities in Marketing Research published by the Marketing Research Association, Inc. (free)

Marketing Communications (monthly), United Business Publications, 475 Park Avenue South, New York, NY 10016

The Marketing News (biweekly), American Marketing Association, 222 South Riverside Plaza, Chicago, IL 60606

Marketing Times (bimonthly), Sales and Marketing Executives International, 330 West 42nd Street, New York, NY 10036

Professional Associations

American Marketing Association
250 South Wacker Drive
Chicago, IL 60606

The Chemical Marketing Research Association
139 Chestnut Avenue
Staten Island, NY 10305

The Life Insurance Marketing Research Association
170 Sigourney Street
Hartford, CT 06105

INTERVIEWS

Tom Keels, Age 29
Research Director
Louis Harris Associates
New York, NY

I got into market research in 1980. After working in publicity at a publishing house, I decided to switch careers. I knew I liked marketing, so I looked at advertising, marketing consulting, and market research. A friend was working at a small research company called Crossely Surveys; he helped me get a part-time job as an editor-coder so I could see if I liked the work. I found it interesting, so when I was offered a job as a project assistant a few months later, I accepted.

I started in an entry-level job because very few skills transfer directly from publicity to market research. I had good writing skills and was comfortable talking on the phone, but these were not important immediately because I wasn't in a position to deal with clients.

As a project assistant I carried out the mechanical details of a particular job. In other words, I made sure the questionnaires were typed, proofed, and sent out to the field. I supervised some interviewing and oversaw editing, coding, and computer cross-tabulation. I remember very clearly one of the first projects I worked on. The client was a major manufacturer of baked goods. We wanted to see if the quality of the packaging could be enhanced, made more attention-getting, by widening the border of the brand-name logo by one-quarter of an inch. A complex scheme was devised in which people were shown slides of new and old packaging in quick succession. If they noticed the new border, we knew it would be a success. Having no idea of what to expect, I was sent to shopping malls to grab shoppers and ask them to look at slides of a cookie package! It was an interesting introduction to research!

The initial excitement of gathering data tends to wear off once you learn basic research techniques. The process is the same whatever product you are investigating. The challenge lies in the analysis, not the actual research.

After a year at Crossely, I moved to AMF, another research company, as project director. I started dealing with clients, usually counterparts at my level; that is, people managing, rather than planning, a study. In mid-1982, I joined Louis Harris Associates as a research associate and was named research director in early 1983. I'm still overseeing detail work—that's something you really can't avoid even when you reach the level of vice president—but I have more creative input. At the end of a study I analyze data, meet with clients to go over results, and write a final report.

I now do a lot of work with banks. The creation of the "financial supermarket" has make the banking industry more conscious of the marketplace. As a result, I've had to learn a lot about finance. Banking is one area where research is just beginning to make inroads, and it's exciting to sell potential clients on the importance of research itself, not just the result of a particular study.

I like the variety that comes from working with a research supplier. You have to be a good juggler because you may be dealing with seven or eight projects at once. I like sitting down with seemingly unrelated data and creating a logical picture from them. But this analysis is interspersed with going out to meet people and sell them on a survey idea. It's not all desk work and it's not all sales; it's a combination of the two. Research provides a chance to use different parts of myself in different ways.

John DeBiassio, Age 35
Vice President
Russell Research
New York, NY

Although I've worked in market research for seven years, my association with it goes back much farther. Before I came to

Russell Research I worked in straight marketing with Progresso Foods. I started at Progresso, working in product management, after getting a master's in business administration. Eventually I became marketing services manager, and in this position I began to get involved with research. The last position I held at Progresso was assistant director of marketing; my functions included being research director. We never conducted any research of our own, but I worked with the research companies who researched the market for us.

I made the switch to market research for a number of reasons. Most of all, I find research fascinating. I also like the fast pace of a research company; it's much more active than straight marketing. The diversity of products to be dealt with was another strong attraction.

My marketing experience has been a valuable factor in my success in research. I came to this profession with a pragmatic approach that resulted from understanding marketing needs. I see beyond the research techniques. This results-oriented viewpoint improves my dealings with clients; I've been in their place and understand their goals.

I've worked on a wide variety of projects, from the simple to the complex. I've tested very specific promotional and advertising materials, such as a tag on clothing. Small details can make a difference in the way the public responds to a product. You must ask: what is the effectiveness of a colored tag versus a black and white one? Of one brand name over another? I've also handled much broader problems—evaluating entire marketing strategies, determining the best packaging, repositioning product lines. Here the questions require more analysis. Does the product live up to consumer expectations? Can it be sold to a specific segment of the market?

A complex project I've worked on was a tourism study for a country that hopes to attract American tourists. The study involved a series of questions: How do Americans perceive this country? Does the country have an image problem in the United States? If so, is it a major problem? How can it be overcome?

Often the results of a particular study show there is a problem—in packaging, advertising, marketing, whatever. Unfortunately, not all clients take this news and our advice as well as we would like. Some will request further research to confirm our findings. Of course, this in never the case when the study has favorable results!

PERSONNEL

THE personnel department is not just a place to turn for information and interviews as you pursue your first job; this department is itself a wonderful source of career options. Whether called by the commonly known term *personnel* or the now widely accepted term *human resources*, this department concerns itself with the human factor of an organization.

Personnel work is a vital part of the business world. It involves much more than screening applicants. Personnel departments are responsible for recruiting the best possible employees, designing compensation and benefits packages for present and retired employees, handling employee labor relations, and overseeing the training and development of employees. People expect more now from an employer than just a job and a weekly paycheck, and the personnel department is there to see that those expectations are met.

The most desirable candidates for personnel work are those who bring an ability to communicate and an acquired knowledge of the business world. Some work experience in that world, preferably in a personnel-related job, is often required of applicants for the most challenging jobs. Many colleges and universities offer degrees in personnel management and labor relations, but plenty of room remains for graduates with liberal arts degrees.

Most entry-level positions are found in large corporations and in employment agencies, but job opportunities in personnel fluctuate. When the economy or a company falls on hard times, general hiring and, consequently, personnel hiring are cut. Personnel is not a revenue-producing department, so it is often the first to experience layoffs and hiring freezes.

On the plus side, keep in mind that now is an exciting time to enter the personnel field. The techniques and practices of this industry are changing as personnel departments are given the initiative to develop new policies and procedures in compensation, employee training, and labor relations. The industry has become so diversified that many large departments are organized very differently than they were ten years ago. But the principal functional areas are still:

- **Employment and Recruitment**
- **Compensation and Benefits**
- **Employee/Labor Relations**

If your first job is with a large corporation, it is likely that you will be rotated throughout the department to expose you to all functions. After this initiation period you will be assigned duties limited to a particular area. This kind of broad exposure can also prepare you for work of greater responsibility in a smaller company where a thorough knowledge of each function is necessary. Large corporations can have personnel departments of a hundred people or more, while the smallest companies may have only one or two people to perform all personnel duties. Duties vary considerably from company to company. As you advance, you may work as a specialist who handles a part of a single function, or as a generalist who deals in many different aspects of the field.

Changes in people's values and desires on the one hand and increased government regulations on the other have led to both diversification and specialization. Compensation programs have become increasingly complex. Computers are used to keep records, to track company resources, and to help design and evaluate new benefit plans.

Job Outlook

Job Openings Will Grow: As fast as average

Competition For Jobs: Keen

New Job Opportunities: These are mostly available in the specialized areas of the field. Knowledge of computer technology and government regulations can be a plus. Technical recruitment, personnel research, and Human Resources Information Systems (HRIS) are growing rapidly. The compensation and benefits field is perhaps the brightest star on the horizon. New forms of compensation and different types of benefits appear each day and will probably continue to appear as the nation's population grows older. The training and development area is also an up-and-coming specialty within the personnel field. Because competition in the marketplace is so stiff, and because of the increasingly technical nature of much work, corporations are finding it necessary to train personnel carefully, not only to do a specific job, but to develop a broad base of skilled employees who will be able to meet the company's changing needs.

Geographic Job Index

Most entry-level jobs are found in or near large cities, where the largest companies and many corporate headquarters are located. Above entry level, there are personnel departments and jobs wherever there are corporations.

Who the Employers Are

PRIVATE INDUSTRY provides a wide variety of opportunities. Most large and medium-size companies have several employees who deal with personnel; companies with 500 employees or more have whole departments with many internal divisions. Although entry-level employees work almost exclusively for large companies, the large companies account for only half the personnel jobs in the country. Smaller companies will hire only experienced people to handle their more limited personnel needs. Private industry tends to pay better than other employers.

GOVERNMENT agencies and departments often have personnel departments. Most federal personnel needs are handled through the Office of Personnel Management, which is headquartered in Washington, DC, and has branch offices in cities throughout the country. Some federal departments, such as the Department of Defense and the Federal Bureau of Investigation, have their own personnel departments. State and local governments also have personnel staffs.

EMPLOYMENT AGENCIES have more entry-level openings but less job security than any other area of personnel work. Some agencies place job-hunters in a variety of jobs, while others specialize in a particular profession, such as high technology, accounting, or publishing. The best opportunities for challenging work lie in the latter type of agency. Here you work almost exclusively with experienced people, trying to match their skills with employers' needs. Some of these agencies have earned wide respect within the industries they serve.

You begin as a counselor, matching job seekers and job openings, lining up interviews, and developing rapport with client companies so they will seek help from you and your agency. Expect to be paid on commission, which can be quite high in the more prestigious, specialized agencies. Experienced counselors may concentrate on executive placement or may train, supervise, and motivate younger counselors. In employment agencies, the energy level is high, the pressure is intense, and the turnover is enormous.

How to Break into the Field

Larger companies offer the best opportunities for inexperienced people. When hiring for their own staffs, personnel departments place an added emphasis on interviews. To demonstrate your ability to work with people and, possibly, to conduct interviews yourself, you must be comfortable and in control in a one-on-one situation. It helps to demonstrate some business savvy, but emphasis should be placed on your organizational and business skills.

Although companies rarely recruit on campus specifically for personnel jobs, you might try scheduling an interview with companies that interest you in order to speak directly to the recruiter about personnel work. Check with your campus placement office for opportunities they may have been apprised of. Entry-level personnel jobs are often advertised in newspapers. You can also write to the personnel director, enclosing a résumé, and follow up your letter with a phone call requesting an interview.

International Job Opportunities

International jobs are limited, even in multinational corporations. Most of them are in training and development.

EMPLOYMENT AND RECRUITMENT

Many times work in the employment area is the first step in a personnel career path. Entry-level employees are often assigned to interview prospective clerical and nonexempt employees. (A nonexempt employee is one who is paid an hourly wage, as opposed to a fixed yearly salary, and is entitled to overtime pay for additional hours worked.) Besides interviewing and recruiting, the employment function deals with hirings, transfers, terminations, retirements, and employee orientation. It also ensures that the company's hiring practices comply with Equal Employment Opportunity (EEO) and Affirmative Action (AA) legislation. Higher-level workers in this area formulate company hiring policies in accordance with this legislation.

For those interested in the employment function, there are also jobs outside the corporate personnel world. Employment agencies, both temporary and permanent, hire and train college graduates as recruiters and interviewers of nonexempt personnel. The work in these agencies is intense and demanding, and the turnover, especially in the lower interviewing positions, is rapid. However, salaries are relatively high and advancement through the company progresses fairly quickly. Many college grads have worked in an agency for up to a year, acquiring the necessary skills to skip working in entry-level recruiting in the corporate world. They then move right into executive recruiting. This is an alternative method of gaining the experience needed for moving up. On the other hand, some corporations frown on such experience. If you enjoy the agency pace, however, you may even find yourself deciding to remain where you are.

Qualifications

Personal: Poise and confidence in yourself. Stamina to carry you through long hours. Ability to make sound judgments on the basis of limited contacts.

Professional: Solid communications and speech skills. Good writing skills. Good interviewing skills.

Career Paths

LEVEL	JOB TITLE	EXPERIENCE NEEDED
Entry	Employment interviewer, nonexempt recruiter	College degree
2	Professional recruiter, EEO/AA specialist	1-2 years
3	Recruitment supervisor, employment supervisor	2-5 years
4	Human resources planning manager, employment manager	4-7 years

Job Responsibilities

Entry Level

THE BASICS: Interviewing clerical applicants and reporting your decisions to supervisors. Administering, grading, and filing pre-employment tests. Processing and doing all paperwork for transfers, hirings, firings, and retirements. Keeping employment records and statistics for future reference.

MORE CHALLENGING DUTIES: Interviewing nonclerical candidates and reporting your opinions to supervisors. Recruiting personnel from colleges. Developing EEO/AA employment plans. Helping supervisors formulate company employment policy.

Moving Up

Higher-level workers either handle executive recruitment and interviewing or formulate company employment policies. Employment managers must make sure that the company's employment policy complies with regulations. They keep in close touch with other departments in an attempt to foresee and prepare for future employment needs. Dealing with the EEO/AA regulations can be extremely complex, and this has led to an increasing number of specialists in this area.

COMPENSATION AND BENEFITS

Of all the areas in a company, the one that most deeply affects everyone is compensation and benefits. Here is where compensation plans and policies for company employees are designed and implemented. Job duties are analyzed and positions evaluated. A considerable amount of record-keeping is involved in this function, and the ability to maintain clear records is imperative.

The variety of employee benefits is growing and the overall field is becoming more sophisticated. New benefits are joining such established perks as insurance and discounts on expensive products made by the company. All employees in a certain category used to be offered the same benefits. Now many companies are willing to tailor benefits to meet individual needs. For example, a worker may be permitted to replace a certain number of sick days with extra vacation time. The department must ascertain whether these options are cost-efficient, whether they are tax liable, and whether they might upset the local salary structure.

The compensation department is responsible for conceiving and administering new compensation plans. Once the plan has been implemented, it's up to this department to evaluate, on a continuing basis, how well it is meeting the needs of the company without wasting the company's resources. Workers in this department sometimes feel they are performing a sort of balancing act. Here is a challenge worthy of a creative mind that is augmented by both a practical streak and a keen sense of detail.

Qualifications

Personal: The patience to work with lots of figures to get needed results. The flexibility to reconcile company and employee wishes. An understanding of what will make employees work harder and produce more.

Professional: Typing or, in some companies, the ability to use a word processor. Good communications skills. Basic mathematical and accounting skills.

Career Paths

LEVEL	JOB TITLE	EXPERIENCE NEEDED
Entry	Personnel assistant	College degree
2	Wage analyst, benefits analyst	2-4 years
3	Benefits administrator, wage administrator	5-7 years

4	Compensation manager, benefits manager	7-10 years

Job Responsibilities

Entry Level

THE BASICS: Keeping company employment records (lots of numbers in rows and columns). Compiling and tallying data for wage and benefits surveys. Writing job descriptions. Conducting company surveys on compensation plans.

MORE CHALLENGING DUTIES: Evaluating job duties. Making suggestions to supervisors on what might be incorporated into compensation plans. Contacting outside parties about new compensation plans. Informing employees how new plans affect them.

Moving Up

As you move up, you will begin to research job descriptions and productivity within the company by speaking with employees and examining records; to determine what changes might be called for and to design specific alterations when they are needed. You may also act as a go-between in times of tension between company and employee. The ability to get along with many types of people is a quality you will need to progress, as well as a cool head and good judgment.

Paperwork lessens as you move up, leaving you more time for substantive work. Travel increases as you visit company branch offices to make sure that new plans are understood and appropriately administered. Higher level workers in this area have a wide latitude in the way they perform their jobs, and also have the satisfaction of seeing the effects of their work on the well-being of the company and its employees.

EMPLOYEE/LABOR RELATIONS

The labor relations area of personnel is responsible for maintaining good relations between a company and its employees and, if necessary, their unions. It investigates all employee complaints and tries to settle them in a fair and consistent manner that conforms to company policy. It also monitors employee behavior in connection with contracts and labor agreements. Enormous amounts of research are needed every time a case comes up. Most of this work is done by entry-level personnel.

Any time problems exist with employees or unions, the labor relations department must represent the company in hearings and at bargaining sessions. But the even more important work is trying to keep a problem from escalating to that level.

Higher-echelon workers in employee/labor relations interpret existing labor laws and formulate appropriate company policy. The department maintains constant communications with other departments within the company to ensure that policies are administered correctly and works closely with the compensation and benefits department.

In smaller organizations, the labor relations area can also be responsible for health and safety considerations. Familiarity with this area is important in contract negotiations.

Qualifications

Personal: Patience with people and paperwork. Tact, diplomacy, and, most important, flexibility. The ability to think on your feet. The ability to work calmly and well under pressure.

Professional: Typing or, in some companies, the ability to use a word processor. Good speech and communications skills.

Career Paths

LEVEL	JOB TITILE	EXPERIENCE NEEDED
Entry	Labor relations specialist	College degree, possible labor relations degree
2	Labor relations supervisor	3-5 years
3	Employee/labor relations manager	8-10 years

Job Responsibilities

Entry Level

THE BASICS: Maintaining records on employee attendance, compliance with contracts, eligibility for insurance and benefits. Doing research and paperwork for individual employee grievance reports. Attending grievance meetings as an assistant. Compiling facts and figures for company labor negotiations.

MORE CHALLENGING DUTIES: Helping superiors prepare for contract negotiations by interviewing employees. Reading and reporting on relevant articles. Investigating complaints within the company. Maintaining close enough contact with people in the company to determine if any problems are brewing.

Moving Up

To move into more responsible positions you will have to demonstrate the ability to deal with many different kinds of people. You will also have to show that you can get groups of people with differing points of view to understand their adversary's thinking and to come to an amicable compromise. This is often difficult work, and you have to be tough enough to withstand the heat of the battle.

Higher-level jobs require not only good judgment and quick, clear thinking, but the ability to handle the mountain of detail work necessitated by employment regulations and increasingly complex corporate structures. To move into a managerial position you will need to be able to supervise workers and delegate responsibility. At the highest levels you will work with executives from other corporate departments to formulate company policy.

ADDITIONAL INFORMATION

Salaries

Salaries in personnel departments vary according to the size and resources of the company. Of the three functional areas, employment and recruitment tends to be the lowest-paying, followed by employee and labor relations. The highest salaries tend to be paid in compensation and benefits.

Entry level	$12,000 to $18,000
Recruiter, analyst, supervisor	$18,000 to $28,000
Supervisor, administrator	$25,000 to $35,000
Manager	$30,000 to $50,000

Working Conditions

Hours: Hours are fairly regular for entry-level employees. Plan on putting in at least an eight-hour day, five days a week. Interviewers must often work through lunch, because that is when many job applicants come in for interviews. Labor relations workers will put in tremendously long hours during contract negotiations.

Environment: Personnel offices tend to be modern and comfortable, because these spaces are seen by job applicants and the public. The larger the company, the more attractive the office.

Workstyle: Work is largely done at your desk, whether you are interviewing applicants, doing a wage survey, or researching a report on employee grievances. During times of major contract negotiations, work in labor relations and in compensation and benefits can be pressured and intense.

Travel: Personnel is not a field that promises much in the way of travel at any level. However, college recruiters visit schools during term time, and compensation and benefits managers may travel to different company outposts to implement new salary or benefit plans. In labor relations there may be some travel at higher levels to company plants or branches for troubleshooting or in preparation for contract negotiations.

Extracurricular Activities/Work Experience

Residence adviser
New student counselor
Admissions office tour guide
Work on school committees, such as student government, that negotiate policy and settle grievances

Internships

There are no formal internships in personnel work. Investigate internship possibilities by contacting personnel departments and expressing your interest. Many are willing to take on interns. Chances are good that you will spend most of your time helping with clerical duties, but you will learn how the department functions and make contacts that will be useful after graduation.

Recommended Reading

BOOKS

Cases and Exercises in Personnel, George S. Stevens and William F. Gluck, eds., Business Publications: 1983

The Personnel Management Game by Jerald R. Smith, Simtek: 1980

PERIODICALS

Personnel Administrator (monthly), American Society for Personnel Administration, 30 Park Drive, Berea, OH 44017

The Personnel Consultant (monthly), 1012 Fourteenth Street, N.W., Washington, DC 20005

Personnel Journal (monthly), 866 West 18th Street, Costa Mesa, CA 92627

Professional Associations

American Society for Personnel Administration
30 Park Drive
Berea, OH 44017

American Society for Training and Development
600 Maryland Avenue, S.W.
Washington, DC 20024

INTERVIEWS

Carolyn Grillo, age 30
Personnel Director, City Investing Co.
New York, NY

I graduated from Yale in 1974 in the second class that had women in it. Because there were only a very few women, I had a lot of opportunities to be on university committees and to watch the administration of a large institution. I majored in organizational psychology and did a lot of work at school with student counseling groups and other student organizations, and I was very interested in what membership in an organization does to a person and what the people in an organization do to it.

When I graduated I went to work at Columbia University, and I quickly found out that I could make almost no contribution unless I understood business. I looked into M.B.A. programs and management training programs at banks. After about a year and a half in Chemical Bank's management training program, I knew that numbers were not my thing, but organizations were, so I volunteered for a job in personnel. So I actually fell into the field. I would have moved into personnel faster if I had taken stock of my skills earlier. I knew coming out of college that I was interested in organizations; I was interested in people's interactions; I inherently had good management skills. And these days, personnel is about management.

I went to City Investing after six years in personnel at Chemical Bank and Merrill Lynch. City Investing is the small parent company of a group of diversified companies with assets of $5 billion. I am what is known as a personnel generalist. I handle recruiting, training, compensation, benefits design and management, employee relations, and management training and development. Those are basically the large areas of personnel. Each is a specialty, and you can spend an entire career in any one of them.

A typical day has some routine maintenance of systems that are already up, some crises, some long-range projects. Personnel jobs like mine can be very reactive. You're fighting fires all day. On a typical day I'll have a manager who wants to fire an employee, has never said anything to the employee about being dissatisfied with him or her, and is at the boiling point; a poor performer who comes in thinking he is being discriminated against because he's a minority person rather than because his performance is poor; an inquiry from a retiree about her benefits coverage; and 60 or 70 letters from new graduates or people still in college who write asking for management training positions. I believe in answering them, which is a massive job in itself.

Some of the letters come handwritten on notebook paper that's been torn out of a loose-leaf. Even some of the typed letters don't impress me, especially the ones that are boisterous and aggressive. The ones I pay attention to give a concise summary of what the people can do, what background they've had. If they've only been in school, I want to know what committees they've been on and what kind of after-school jobs they've had, especially anything meaningful they've done in their work experience. I will almost never consider someone who has never had a part-time job.

What I'm not crazy about in my job is the old image of personnel—friendly people who like people. I can't tell you how many people I've interviewed who when I ask, "Why do you want to work in personnel?" by saying, "I love working with people." My answer is: "Do you like firing people? Do you like disciplining people? Do you like telling people no? Do you like telling people this doesn't make sense, you can't do it?"

What I like about personnel is that every transaction requires judgment. You have to think: Is this fair? Is it equitable? Does it make sense? Also, in a company as small as the one I'm in, I know that if I'm not there I will be missed. Even in larger companies you know when you're working on compensation that you're actually affecting what people are going to be able to earn, and when you're working on recruiting you're actually affecting who's going to get a job and who isn't—and more important than that, whether the company's going to have high-quality employees. I guess what I like most is knowing that I'm making a difference in real people's real lives.

Larry Brochhausen, age 36
Assistant Vice President, Training and Development
Home Insurance Company, New York, NY

I went to Queens College in New York City where I majored in theater and broadcasting. From there, after deciding not to starve to death, I worked in the retail industry and later went to work for the Internal Revenue Service, where I served in a number of increasingly responsible jobs—revenue officer, administrative intern, a training methods specialist, chief of training at the Andover, MA, service center, and operations branch manager at Andover. From that job I moved into the senior analyst position for that service center, overseeing productivity and resources. I did all the scheduling for the work that was done. At that point, after 11 years of service, I decided that the federal government did not offer the long-range opportunities that I wanted, and I came to the Home Insurance Company in operations. After about four weeks my predecessor in this job left the organization. Because Home Insurance knew of my training and development background, they asked me if I would be interested in the promotion.

Primarily I am responsible for all the training activities that go on in the company, with the exception of computer or MIS training. I have a staff of eight. We train people in the technical skills involved in casualty/property insurance. We're responsible for identifying the training needs, designing course material to meet those needs, and training technical people to be instructors. We're also responsible for management training and a marketing program to train sales personnel.

It seems that no day is really typical. Most of my time is divided between overseeing my staff, reviewing materials, looking at approaches that we will take on a given project. I am less a trainer now and more a project manager. Like any other manager, I serve as a buffer for my people primarily with the higher-level human resources management, as well as sometimes with the technical management. We have one other major program in the company, which is an intern program where we bring in fast-track people—M.B.A.s usually or business majors. It's a seven-and-a-half year program, highly visible in the company. We spend a great deal of time handling individual intern problems, monitoring their progress. We're responsible for watching their salaries and the types of assignments they get.

With the advances in technology and the greater need to be competitive these days, companies need the skills of very good people. The training and development organization provides those skills. Training is becoming more and more a part of management's thinking. Sometimes in the past it might have been an afterthought—we'll hire these people and put them in some kind of training course. But now training is becoming more and more a part of the planning process. When a problem arises in the organization, very often training is called on to be at least part of the solution. Part of our job is to say when training is not the solution, when something is an operational or systemic problem, as opposed to a skill problem. There's just no doubt that training is now an integral part of how an operation runs. Effective training is very costly, and you need to have the most expertise available in your training and development department to reduce that cost and to make the training as efficient as possible. What I like about training—and maybe this is a parochial view—as opposed to a lot of the human resources-type functions is that training is the area that gives you the most flexibility, the most creativity. We are not bogged down by and don't have to get involved in a lot of processes, a lot of numbers. We get involved in providing solutions,and the more creative we can be in those solutions, as long as creativity includes efficiency and effectiveness, the better we're doing our jobs.

PUBLIC RELATIONS

WHEN you talk up a new movie, are your friends eager to see it? Did you persuade your entire dorm to donate blood? Were you able to draft a petition that got a favorable response? If you have a talent for getting others enthused about your interests and convinced about your beliefs, then public relations may be an excellent field in which to build a career.

Public relations, or PR, is communicating to the public on behalf of a client or company—to advocate a position, introduce a new product or service, build a positive image. Any person or group that wants to command and keep people's attention will turn to a public relations professional. Your firm, or department if you work within a corporation, may be called upon to promote a director's latest movie or unveil a new computer model, to talk to legislators on behalf of a manufacturing group, or to explain a recent change in corporate policy to employees.

A college degree is the only absolute requirement for an entry-level job in public relations, because there's a great deal of learning on the job. Communications and journalism majors often have an edge, because of the number and variety of communications courses they have taken, but liberal arts majors with strong writing credentials are also welcome. Although only a limited number of colleges offer a public relations major (one of the best preparations for the field), many have public relations courses available through their communications departments.

Good speaking skills are also vital in this field, and experience in various media—print, broadcast, film, and video—is useful as well. Those who rise to high-level positions often have an advanced degree in the area in which they do public relations work—for example, a master of public administration for those involved in government, or an M.B.A. for those who work in the communications department of a major corporation.

Public relations may be divided into seven areas of specialization, each determined by the audience (or "public") reached. Depending on their size, their clients, and the nature of their companies, public relations agencies and departments may focus on one area or work in all of them. These areas are divided as follows:

Consumer affairs handles inquiries from customers, prepares educational materials, and addresses issues affecting consumers, such as price increases, product quality and safety, warranties and guarantees, and complaints.

Government relations works with legislators and staff in government agencies to make your client's position heard. You may also research, evaluate, and suggest legislation important to your client.

Investor (stockholder) relations prepares reports and statements, handles shareholder inquiries, arranges meetings for stockholders and investors, serves as liaison between investors and management, and encourages investments in your client's company.

Employee relations coordinates contact between employees and management, writes and edits internal publications (often called house organs), arranges in-house seminars and conferences, and explains new company policies.

Community relations maintains good relations between your client and the local community, which often includes government agencies, civic groups, schools, neighborhood boards, block associations, and individuals. This is often done through organized programs and activities, classes, tours of your facility, and publications.

International relations presents your client to the international community, prepares information for use in foreign countries, does research on customs for your client's use, and entertains visiting businesspeople or dignitaries.

Media relations garners favorable media exposure for your client by writing and sending out press releases, arranging press conferences, placing film or video clips, and arranging interviews and appearances.

Regardless of the kind of public you and your employer reach, it's likely that you will be involved in several of the following kinds of work.

- **Research**
- **Program Work**
- **Writing and Editing**
- **Special Events**
- **Media Placement**
- **Public Speaking**
- **Fund Raising**

New technology has begun to affect the way PR professionals gather and disseminate information. Using computers for data retrieval and storage has led to increased efficiency in research, media listing and scheduling, and general office tasks. Word processors are often used for writing and editing. Corporate video systems for teleconferencing (live, telecast meetings involving people in different locations) are becoming more common.

Job Outlook

Job Openings Will Grow: About as fast as average

Competition For Jobs: Keen

New Job Opportunities: New communications technology and the increasing numbers of organizations, businesses, and institutions that are turning to media to gain visibility have created more opportunities in public relations. Recent growth in consumer awareness, government regulations, and new business startups have all increased the need for communication among businesses, public interest groups, and the general public.

Individuals with proven research and writing abilities are in high demand at present. Corporations are also placing a greater emphasis on international public relations; graduates who are fluent in a foreign language, have studied international relations, or, ideally, have lived abroad are sought by firms that handle international PR. Growing high-tech fields, particularly the computer and electronics industries, are looking for recent graduates who are enthusiastic about and have some knowledge of the business applications of computers.

Geographic Job Index

More than half of all American public relations firms (some 2000 companies) are located in New York, NY, and Chicago, IL. Jobs can also be found in other large cities such as Los Angeles, CA, and Washington, DC, where press services and media are easily accessible, and where business and trade associations are headquartered. Because of the wide variety of employers who use public relations professionals, however, entry-level jobs exist in virtually any medium-size city or college town nationwide.

Who the Employers Are

PUBLIC RELATIONS FIRMS service both business and nonprofit clients. Many of the more than 4000 firms nationwide are small, employing fewer than a dozen people. The largest employ more than a hundred people. The larger the firm, the more varied its accounts.

ADVERTISING AGENCY RELATED PR FIRMS are similar in structure and type of accounts to the large PR firms. Ten of the top 50 public relations firms are subsidiaries of ad agencies.

IN-HOUSE PUBLIC RELATIONS DEPARTMENTS of corporations spend billions of dollars annually on public relations. Fortune 1000 companies usually have a staff devoted exclusively to public relations work. Staffs at the largest companies number over a hundred people. Most departments, however, consist of a half dozen people or fewer. Small companies often assign public relations work to their advertising or sales staff. In-house departments are often called communications departments rather than PR departments.

TRADE ASSOCIATIONS. of which there are some 14,000, employ a number of people with public relations skills, even though their staffs are usually small. Most associations work for only one client or a group of clients who share the same interests.

GOVERNMENT AGENCIES at the federal, state, and local levels employ many public information officers. Positions with the federal government must be applied for through the Office of Personnel Management. State and local governments have their own hiring offices.

COLLEGES AND UNIVERSITIES hire PR professionals to promote their school's image in order to boost endowments and increase admissions. Public relations personnel are employed in the campus press relations office, the alumni office, and the development (fund-raising) office.

NONPROFIT ORGANIZATIONS include volunteer agencies in the health, recreation, rehabilitation, and family service areas; hospitals; and youth, community, and religious organizations. These organizations offer opportunities to work for a worthy cause in a less-pressured working environment—but at a lower salary.

LABOR UNIONS at the local, state, national, and international levels employ PR specialists to operate their news bureaus, sponsor radio and television programming, offer films and educational programs, organize speakers' bureaus, and produce publications promoting their viewpoints.

Major Employers

PUBLIC RELATIONS FIRMS

Daniel J. Edelman, Chicago, IL
Fleishman-Hillard, St. Louis, MO
Rogers & Cowan, New York, NY
The Rowland Company, New York, NY
Ruder, Finn & Rotman, New York, NY

ADVERTISING AGENCY AFFILIATED PR FIRMS

Burson-Marsteller, New York, NY
Carl Byoir & Associates, New York, NY
Doremus & Company, New York, NY
Hill and Knowlton, New York, NY
Ketchum Public Relations, Pittsburgh, PA

CORPORATIONS WITH LARGE IN-HOUSE PUBLIC RELATIONS DEPARTMENTS

Exxon Corporation, New York, NY
General Motors Corporation, Detroit, MI
IBM Corporation, White Plains, NY
E.I. Du Pont de Nemours & Company, Wilmington, DE
Proctor & Gamble, Cincinnati, OH

NONPROFIT ORGANIZATIONS

American Cancer Society, New York, NY
American Red Cross, Washington, DC
American Youth Hostels, Washington, DC
The Ford Foundation, New York, NY
The Salvation Army, New York, NY

How to Break into the Field

Get practical experience while you're still in college; there are many opportunities to gain exposure and relevant experience. Working summers, part-time, or full-time as a reporter, copy editor, advertising copywriter, or tour guide, or in any other public relations-related capacity, will give you an edge over other candidates.

Start your job campaign armed with a list of potential employers, and a stack of résumés and writing samples. It's fine to write or call a senior person in an agency or department, but in the case of small agencies, it pays simply to show up and ask to speak to the president. Showing initiative and confidence can make the difference in your landing a position. If you can sell yourself, employers will see you as a promising prospect.

THE WORK

An entry-level position is comparable to an apprenticeship. You assist experienced people, handling the detail work and learning by doing. In a large public relations firm, you will progress through a well-defined career path. However, no defined path exists in a very small firm (one to six people). In a small organization or company, the public relations or communications director and an assistant may comprise the entire department. As a PR professional, you may be involved in one or more of the following functions, depending on your skills and experience, and the needs of your employer.

RESEARCH must be done before any PR campaign can begin to determine the client's objectives, how their competition has handled a similar project, and how best to accomplish the goals. Research work may include interviews, library research, conducting surveys, and consultation with firms specializing in opinion research. As an entry-level person, you'll probably be involved more in research than in any other PR function. You will start with basic fact-finding—determining the opinions and attitudes of people likely to be influenced by your client's programs, products, or policies. With experience, you will be asked to interpret and evaluate research data, as well as to gather it.

PROGRAM WORK is another area of involvement. As soon as enough research is collected, the results are analyzed. Often the client's objectives and goals are redefined, new audiences are pinpointed, or the budget is reevaluated. Then a program of activities and events—a strategy—is planned to win support, create opportunities for exposure, or otherwise influence the target audience.

WRITING AND EDITING is part of virtually every PR campaign. In addition to the internal memos and reports circulated among staff during the research and programming stage, written presentations must be made to the clients, letters must be written to people whose endorsement or support is important to the campaign, and press releases must be widely circulated. To get results, writing must be clear, concise, and persuasive. Plenty of writing and editing is part of the daily activities of PR professionals who work for one client, including working on film scripts, trade magazine articles, product information releases, employee publications, newsletters, and shareholder reports. Although most PR staff members aren't required to have a lot of production know-how, that is, expertise in printing, layout, typography, or film processing—familiarity with these functions is an asset.

SPECIAL EVENTS that are carefully staged and planned to attract the attention of the public you want to reach are frequently part of a PR campaign. Even if everyone in your target group cannot actually attend the event, you may be able to reach a much wider group through media coverage of it, if the event is unique, visually exciting, or otherwise appealing to a mass audience. Special events may be as serious as a news conference or as entertaining as an anniversary rock concert, but in any case they require detailed preparation from planning to promotion to staging.

MEDIA PLACEMENT, which includes selecting information to be released, the media contacts to receive it, and the timing of the release, is crucial to the success of a campaign. Convincing the press to cover your story and persuading them to present it in a favorable way is also part of the job. This means being persistent but not aggressive and having friendly relationships with members of the press. Information that might be promoted to the media as news or feature stories include the release of a new drug by a pharmaceutical company, a corporation's quarterly earnings report, a celebrity's comeback, or a senator's bid for reelection. PR spokespersons, particularly those for corporations, are sometimes called upon to soften the impact of news that could damage their client's image.

PUBLIC SPEAKING, that is, making presentations in front of a group, is not a frequently called upon skill in most public relations departments. Still, it's an asset that you can capitalize on with experience. Knowing how to address a group effectively or how to handle yourself in front of a TV camera or microphone might enable you eventually to become a spokesperson for a client or your company.

FUNDRAISING is an important function in nonprofit organizations, such as trade associations, labor unions, foundations, and special-interest organizations. Fund-raising techniques include direct mail solicitation, benefit events (balls, dinners,), radio and television appeals, marathons, door-to-door canvassing, and membership drives. Fundraising requires an in-depth knowledge of the client's constituency, strong organizational skills, good interpersonal skills. A personal belief in your client's work helps as well.

Qualifications

Personal: Enthusiasm. Ability to solve problems creatively. Strong interpersonal skills. Ability to work as a member of a team. Persuasiveness. Sensitivity to current trends and issues.

Professional: Strong research and writing skills. Public speaking skill. Understanding of how the media works.

Career Paths

LEVEL	JOB TITLE	EXPERIENCE NEEDED
Entry	Assistant account executive or trainee	College degree. Some PR experience preferred
2	Account executive	2-5 years
3	Account supervisor	5-8 years
4	Vice president or account services or director	10+ years

Job Responsibilities

Entry Level

THE BASICS: Maintain files. Type. Answer phones. Scan and clip newspaper and magazine articles. Research and assemble information for speeches and pamphlets. Prepare media lists.

MORE CHALLENGING DUTIES: Write press releases, short articles for employee publications, and business correspondence. Direct information and story ideas to media contacts. Handle details for special events—travel arrangements, making sure VIPs are met and welcomed, following up on RSVP's.

Moving Up

How fast you move from being the office assistant to being a full-fledged account executive depends on the size of the firm or department. Promotions will depend on your ability to contribute to the success of a campaign, to generate innovative ideas, and to follow through on assignments. As you prove yourself to be competent and able to handle clients on your own, you will be given your own accounts or, if you're in an in-house PR department, allowed to work with other departments without supervision. Charm and an ability to work well with a wide variety of people will help you move up. Those who make it to the level of account supervisor assume financial responsibility for groups of accounts and coordinate major campaigns. Top managers review budgets and programs, supervise staff, and court new business.

ADDITIONAL INFORMATION

Salaries

Professionals who work for public relations firms or industrial manufacturers and conglomerates earn more than their colleagues who work for other types of employers, and nonprofit organizations pay the lowest salaries. Entry-level annual pay ranges from $10,000 to $16,000. An account executive may earn between $18,000 and $35,000, depending on the size of his or her employer and the type of accounts handled. An account supervisor may earn a salary as high as $60,000. The directors of top PR firms are paid as much as $150,000.

Working Conditions

Hours: Overtime is common, especially when a major campaign is being launched. Many special events are staged in the evening and on weekends, and you'll be required to be there if needed. More regular hours are kept at in-house PR departments. As you move up work tends to spill into personal time—business dinners, press luncheons, and after-work meetings.

Environment: PR firms large and small maintain attractive offices. In-house corporate PR departments are usually quite comfortable, while the offices of those who work for nonprofit organizations and government agencies usually reflect the wealth, or lack of it, of their employers. The environment of PR firms in particular is active and bustling, with phones ringing and visitors coming in and out frequently.

Workstyle: Some days are spent mainly on the phone, others at a typewriter or word processor, others in meetings with senior-level people or clients, or a combination of the three.

Travel: Travel to exciting locations usually comes with clients who can afford lavish affairs or whose business involves travel to choice cities. Senior people always get the glamorous assignments over more junior personnel.

Extracurricular Activities/Work Experience

Campus development office—fund raising

Campus or local newspaper, radio or television station—writing, editing, promotion, sales

College admissions office—working as a tour guide or recruiter

Local, state, or federal political groups—canvassing for a candidate, advocating a ballot issue

Student activities office—planning campus events, coordinating publicity, contacting lecture bureaus and agents

Internships

Individual chapters of the Public Relations Society of America sponsor internships. These programs vary according to chapter. Contact chapters directly; a list is available from the PRSA.

Recommended Reading

BOOKS

Getting Back to the Basics in Public Relations and Publicity by Matthew J. Culligan & Dolph Greene, Crown Publishers: 1982

Lesly's Public Relations Handbook, by Philip Lesly, 3rd ed. Prentice-Hall: 1983

O'Dwyer's Directory of Corporate Communications by J. R. O'Dwyer, J. R. O'Dwyer Company: 1982 (lists corporate public relations departments, geographic index)

O'Dwyer's Directory of Public Relations Firms by J. R. O'Dwyer, J. R. O'Dwyer Company: 1983 (lists public relations firms, addresses and clients, geographic index)

The Practice of Public Relations by Wilfrid Howard, David & Charles: 1982

Publicity for Volunteers: A Handbook by Virginia Bortin, Walker & Company: 1981

PERIODICALS

PR Reporter (weekly), PR Publishing Company, Inc., Box 600, Dudley House, Exeter, NH 03833

Publicist (bimonthly), Public Relations Aids, Inc., 330 West 34th Sreet., New York, NY 10001

Public Relations News (weekly), 127 East 80th Street, New York, NY 10021

Public Relations Quarterly (quarterly), 44 West Market Street, P.O. Box 311, Rhinebeck, NY 12572

For a complete bibliography of Public Relations publications, send $10 prepaid to:

PRSA Information Center
845 Third Avenue 12th Floor
New York, NY 10022

Professional Associations

International Association of Business Communicators
870 Market Street
San Francisco, CA 94102

International Communication Association (ICA)
Balcones Research Center
10100 Burnet Road
Austin, TX 78758

National School of Public Relations Association
1801 North Moore Street
Arlington, VA 22209

Public Relations Society of America
845 Third Avenue
New York, NY 10022

INTERVIEWS

Vivian Manuel, Age 42
President
VM Communications, Inc., New York, NY

I'm the only daughter in my family, and I always remember being told that I could be whatever I wanted to be. I went to Wells College in Aurora, NY, majored in biology, and went on to graduate work in political science at the University of Wyoming.

After a stint as a service representative at Mountain States Telephone & Telegraph in Denver, I went to Washington, DC, where I ended up working as a professional political fund raiser. That led to a job as a management analyst in the staff office of the Secretary of the Navy. One of my assignments was to help military people improve communications with the public; another was to act as a civilian liaison with other federal agencies. It was during this time that I became interested in public relations as a profession. For me, that meant New York!

So in 1968 I applied for a job at General Electric Company's New York corporate office. They offered me one as a junior publicist. At first I handled consumer electronics account work and was able to use the skills I'd learned in Washington. I subsequently worked on a project named Tektite (a research program conducted in an underwater habitat built by GE) and the Apollo space program (GE provided the power pack flown to the moon to power experiments). I was responsible for keeping the press up-to-date and translating scientific data into layperson's terms. Both experiences taught me that PR is more hard work than glamour.

In 1972 I was named press representative, business/finance—the first woman to hold that particular corporate position. My job involed everything from handling company's earnings and dividends to broad actions affecting stockholder interests. One of the biggest challenges was working as GE's media contact during the complex Hudson River PCB pollution case.

Although this was a rewarding job and a great learning experience, I wanted to deal with a variety of issues and industries and the urge to "do it myself" seemed the answer. I formed VM Communications and specialized in financial, stockholder, and employee communications. My firm handles issues management, product publicity, corporate analysis, program design, and implementation. This means we find answers on how to communicate on many subjects and issues, from product boycotts and strikes to bad weather to the price of a client's stock.

It's not always fun—the hours are long, the administrative chores many, but the rewards are great. PR is really bringing together the "business of business" with the "business of the public," so they can better communicate with each other. I'm still learning, that's for sure. And I love what I do.

John Springer
President
John Springer Associates, Inc., New York, NY

When I got out of college I went back to Rochester, NY, where I had grown up, as a movie and theater critic for a local radio station. The station would send me to New York City once every few months to review new plays and interview stars. Those were the days when the movie studios in New York would roll out the red carpet for any visiting press, even a kid from Rochester. I got to know people at the studios very well, and they began to offer me jobs in their public relations departments. I had never meant to get into movie publicity. I always thought that I would be a theater and film writer and critic. But the idea of living in New York and making good money was a big lure, so I finally accepted a publicity job with RKO Pictures.

For 16 years I worked in various companies before I started my own PR firm. I had many opportunities to go on my own during that time, but I always resisted them. I was making very good money working for other people, and I knew many people who had gone on their own and fallen on their faces. But people kept bugging me and I finally decided to start my own office.

I started with five clients: Henry Fonda, Warren Beatty, Robert Preston, Richard Burton, and Hal Prince. And then within three weeks I also had Elizabeth Taylor, Tony Randall, and Mike Nichols. I like the personal contact work that is inherent in my business. The people I represent range from a 7-year-old girl, Drew Barrymore, to a 77-year-old great lady, Myrna Loy. When I started my own company, I decided I would only represent people I liked and whose talent I respected. It's bound to work better than if you don't.

I have a very close relationship with my clients—much more than a purely professional one. I believe public relations brings important people and worthwhile projects to the public via the media. For example, we presented the one-night showing of the reconstructed Judy Garland film, *A Star is Born*. The attention given this showing brought a sell-out crowd and considerable amounts of money for the Preservation Program of the Academy of Motion Picture Arts and Sciences.

There are tremendous pressures in public relations work. For example, one day I might have a big show opening and the press contacts might fall through for one reason or another. That can be harrowing and aggravating. Or I might pick up *The New York Times* looking for a story I thought was all set and, for whatever reason, something else has replaced it. Disappointments are standard in public relations, but the rewards are exhilarating.

REAL ESTATE

TRADITIONALLY, the real estate industry has attracted many homemakers and retirees who wanted flexible hours and the opportunity to make extra income. But today an increasing number of college graduates are choosing real estate as a full-time profession. In addition to bringing together buyers and sellers of property, real estate professionals are increasingly involved in more complex activities, such as sophisticated development and leasing enterprises, property management, and commercial appraisal.

Graduates will find opportunities in the following areas:

- **Sales**
- **Appraisal**
- **Property management**

Like the stock market, the real estate market is cyclical. When interest rates are low, mortgages become more affordable, construction loans more available, and consequently, more transactions take place. The prognosis for job opportunities in this field is very good throughout the eighties. The most geographically mobile group in the population, and the one that traditionally makes the majority of home purchases, is the 22-to-35-year olds. During the current decade many of the 1950's baby boom generation will become potential home buyers. Furthermore, since so many people in this group are well educated, their earnings will continue to rise; they can be expected to buy larger homes and more vacation properties.

Although residential real estate transactions are the more numerous, commercial real estate transactions are usually the more lucrative. In the early 1980s, a 23-year-old woman named Ellen Israel, who had less than a year's experience in real estate, negotiated the $40-million sale of a Manhattan office tower. She shared the $500,000 commission on the sale with the licensed broker who helped her and the company for which she worked. Most commercial deals are not as spectacular as that one and are achieved only after years of acquiring negotiating skills, but some industry experts maintain that commercial real estate offers better opportunities for entry-level people to learn the brokerage business than does residential real estate.

Computer technology is revolutionizing the industry. Now, clients' requirements can be fed into a terminal and relevant listings called up. Because of the number of cross-references and listings that can easily be maintained, brokers and salespeople save hours and even days of work. The computer can also quickly provide follow-up reports and property updates, allowing more thorough and efficient service.

If you want to become a broker, the type of degree you've earned isn't as important as your initiative and sales ability. Many consider sales the most challenging and lucrative area of real estate. The most successful brokers are people who possess excellent communications skills, an entrepreneurial spirit—and a broker's license. One liability for recent graduates who are considering sales is that you may have to forgo income for as long as six months after you begin working, since most employers do not pay a salary. Earnings are based on commissions from listings and sales.

A bachelor's degree in business or a strong core of business courses is helpful if you plan to go into some of the more technical areas of real estate, such as commercial appraisal or development.

Job Outlook

Job Openings Will Grow: Much faster than average

Competition for Jobs: Some
Expect the most competition for the more technical jobs, particularly those available at commercial banks.

New Job Opportunities: Real estate has become part of the world of high finance. Brokerage firms, most notably Merrill Lynch, have instituted their own real estate affiliates. Property now competes with stocks and bonds as a form of investment. A piece of property bought solely for its investment potential has the same status as a security. The investment is originated (financed), managed, and resold for maximum profit through the process known as syndication. This is a sophisticated area for which an M.B.A. is often a prerequisite. Still, it is possible to acquire the necessary knowledge of this function through sales work.

Geographic Job Index

Employment opportunities exist wherever there are properties—houses, office buildings, stores, farms, factories, retirement developments, and resorts. Commercial real estate firms are most often located in major cities. The dense population and large numbers of businesses in cities creates brisk competition for both residential and commercial sites and consequently a high rate of turnover. A majority of the major finance companies are located in cities as well, facilitating real estate transactions.

Who the Employers Are

NATIONAL REAL ESTATE FIRMS AND FRANCHISES usually specialize in either commercial or residential sales, although some of the largest ones handle both. A firm is a single company with agency branches, while a franchise leases its name, training program, and advertising to independent agencies who want to be affiliated with a recognized company. (Century 21 is one of the largest such franchises.) A real estate firm usually hires from a central office, while each local franchise does its own hiring.

LOCAL AND REGIONAL REALTY FIRMS are small, often family-owned agencies that primarily handle residential and small commercial transactions.

APPRAISAL COMPANIES specialize in evaluating the market value of buildings and property, both commercial and residential. They offer fewer jobs than do real estate firms, but are growing in number.

MANAGEMENT FIRMS administer and manage property, primarily commercial property. Many specialize in one type of establishment—apartment buildings, office buildings, resorts, or commercial holdings.

BANKS AND BROKERAGE HOUSES are hiring an increasing number of people to handle appraisals, syndications, and development. They often look for candidates with specific financial skills or with a year or two of experience in some real estate specialty.

Major Employers

COMMERCIAL REAL ESTATE FIRMS

Arthur Rubloff & Co., Chicago, IL
Coldwell Banker, Los Angeles, CA
Cushman & Wakefield, New York, NY
Grubb & Ellis, Oakland, CA
Merrill Lynch Realty, New York, NY

RESIDENTIAL REAL ESTATE FIRMS AND FRANCHISES

Beard & Warner, Chicago, IL
Century 21, Irvine, CA
Henry S. Miller, Dallas, TX
Shannon & Luchs, Washington, DC
Van Schaack & Company, Denver, CO

How to Break into the Field

Very few real estate firms recruit on campus, but it's worth finding out if any plan to visit your school's placement office. Although few universities offer a real estate curriculum, many offer real estate courses through their adult or continuing education divisions. You cannot earn degree credit by taking one or more of these courses, but you often can earn continuing education credits that will help you fulfill the requirements for a sales license. Most states require candidates for the general sales license to complete at least 30 hours of classroom instruction. You must then take an examination, which includes questions on basic real estate transactions and on laws affecting the sale of property. In general it takes six months to get a license (assuming you pass the test), because classes usually meet for a few hours once or twice a week.

The best way to identify potential employers in a particular area is to check the Yellow Pages under Residential or Commercial Real Estate. The office or institute that administers the real estate program often has information about local employers.

Most real estate firms require entry-level salespeople to have a sales license or at least to be enrolled in a preparatory program. The best way to land a sales spot is to set up an interview with the manager of a firm. How well you sell yourself in the interview will be the major factor in the decision to hire you as a salesperson.

International Job Possibilities

Although some American real estate firms have branches abroad, most of the jobs there would be filled by nationals who have better contacts and knowledge of client needs. Appraisers and developers are the kinds of real estate professionals who are most likely to be called on by foreign businesses to work outside the United States.

SALES

At one time, an experienced broker would sit a new salesperson down, point to the telephone, and expect results. Success depended largely on personal contacts and bravado. These assets are still a boon, but now they're only the beginning. A successful sale depends on a series of skillfully executed steps.

First you must seek out newly available real estate that is appropriate for the company's listings (e.g., commercial or residential; high-, middle-, or low-income; urban, suburban, or rural). You then follow up by personally inspecting the property. If it is suitable, you must secure the owner's agreement to list with your firm. In the face of competition from other real estate companies that want to list the property, you will have to try to persuade the owner that the property should be listed exclusively with your firm.

Matching clients with listings usually entails many hours of showing properties, getting to know your clients better, and learning how to meet the individual's needs or—in the commercial market—the client company's needs.

In commercial real estate the most important considerations—aside from price, which is always a key factor—are size, location, prestige, and proximity to transportation. Although the client may have very specific requirements in all these areas, a skilled salesperson who understands the market knows how to present worthwhile alternatives. In the residential market individuals also have strong ideas about what type of property they want and how much they can spend, but their final choice often depends on how they feel about the house. A family, for example, may want a house that is near a school, off the main road, and within walking distance of a shopping center. If none of your listings quite fills the bill, it's up to you to spot the client's weakness for, say, southern exposures, fireplaces, and a yard with trees. You may have a property with a strong appeal for the client even though it doesn't satisfy all of the initial criteria.

A new and important aspect of residential sales is relocation management. Some large firms train salespeople to deal with clients who are moving to one area of the country from another. They give clients advice above and beyond the financial aspects of buying a particular property, e.g., which schools or school districts are desirable, what churches, social, and community groups are in the area. In fact, firms specializing in relocation counseling and management are growing in number. Moving can be a traumatic experience for some members of a family, and many relocation firms are headed by psychologists, but they also employ people whose strong point is a good knowledge of the social, cultural, and recreational aspects of the community. The biggest customers of relocation firms are major corporations that are transferring employees from one business location to another.

Some salespeople are better at attracting listings than they are at closing a deal; others have the reverse strengths. As a result, salespeople sometimes put their efforts into one area or the other. If you find that you excel in obtaining listings, don't worry about missing out on sales commissions. It's common practice now for the person obtaining the listing to share in the commission.

Qualifications

Personal: Entrepreneurial instincts. Resourcefulness and enthusiasm. Ability to relate to many different types of people. Self-confidence. Perseverance. Good listening skills.

Professional: Sales license. Good math skills. Sales savvy.

Career Paths

LEVEL	JOB TITLE	EXPERIENCE NEEDED
Entry	Salesperson or trainee	Sales experience preferred
2	Broker	College degree a plus, 1-3 years
3	Firm manager or owner	5+ years

Job Responsibilities

Entry Level

THE BASICS: Being on floor duty—answering phones, fielding calls for other brokers. Checking newspaper listings for accuracy. In the field, looking for possible properties.

MORE CHALLENGING DUTIES: Showing properties. Doing financial analyses of potential buyers. Negotiating deals between buyers and sellers.

Moving Up

As a salesperson, you'll be working under the auspices of a broker, whose participation is necessary to close a transaction officially. After you have worked for one to three years (depending on the regulations in your state) and have taken 90 hours of formal training, you'll be eligible to take an exam to become a broker. (If you have a bachelor's degree in real estate, you may be able to get the experience requirement waived.) In sales, the only thing that separates the beginner from the successful broker is experience. The more transactions you're involved in and the more varied the kinds of properties you deal with, the more you'll learn about the business.

APPRAISAL

Appraisers determine market prices for properties ranging from tiny residential plots to vast industrial tracts. Real estate appraisal used to be done primarily by banks, which assessed the worth of a given property when it was being bought or sold by a customer. Offices specializing in this real estate function are sprouting up nationwide, both as independent firms and as divisions of banks. It is becoming a vastly diversified field, involving, in addition to property appraisal, cost analyses for banks, feasibility studies for developers, evaluations of joint ventures between banks, principals and developers, and other related functions.

Appraisers do not need a sales license, but they must take a series of classes and exams to qualify them in different market areas. These are not required for a first job, but appraisers are expected to enroll soon after being hired. Many real estate firms—again, depending on their size—have appraisers on their staffs.

The most significant credential in appraisal is the M.A.I. (Member Appraisal Institute) designation, given by the American Institute of Real Estate Appraisers. Although this credential isn't required, anyone with ambition will pursue it. Only M.A.I. will give you the credibility to go after the most profitable and prestigious accounts. Anywhere from five to ten years of classes and experience are needed to qualify for the exam, at which point you must also produce two demonstration appraisals for evaluation. There are other credentials, too—for example, the S.R.P.A. (senior real property appraiser)—but none of them is as prestigious or as difficult to acquire as the M.A.I.

Qualifications

Personal: An eye for detail. A problem-solving mentality. Willingness to make decisions.

Professional: Good writing skills. Analytical ability. Familiarity with specialized real estate markets and trends.

Career Paths

LEVEL	JOB TITLE	EXPERIENCE NEEDED
Entry	Junior appraiser	College degree, business background preferred
2	Appraiser	2-4 years
3	Senior appraiser	5-8 years
4	Partner	8-10 years

Job Responsibilities

Entry Level

THE BASICS: Fielding questions from clients. Maintaining files on financial trends and existing accounts.

MORE CHALLENGING DUTIES: Appraising single-family residences. Gathering data (inspecting land deeds and records of transactions that might reflect land value). Doing research and writing report.

Moving Up

The longer you're on the job, the more time you can expect to spend doing on-site evaluation, such as appraising "distressed property" values. During your first years you'll be preparing for your M.A.I., which means taking classes and developing a reputation for being a thorough researcher and good judge of property values. Unlike in sales, you can count on more individual attention from the people higher than you, as your work will reflect on them and the company.

PROPERTY MANAGEMENT

As apartment complexes expand, condominiums sprout up, and shopping centers continue to spread in the suburbs and beyond, management of these buildings and units becomes an increasingly important function. Management includes overseeing the physical upkeep of the property, smoothing tenant and community relations, orchestrating rentals and lease renewals, and attending to advertising and the many other duties involved in operating an active property. Although it is not strictly required, most management personnel do possess a sales license, often because they started in sales. However, when management agencies take over the responsibility of leasing properties for their principals, the license becomes crucial.

Qualifications

Personal: Problem-solving mentality. Outgoing personality. Ability to work with all types of people. Willingness to take charge.

Professional: Financial background. Administrative skills. Organization skills. Computer know-how. Awareness of local politics.

Career Paths

LEVEL	JOB TITLE	EXPERIENCE NEEDED
Entry	Trainee or administrative assistant	College degree, business background perferred
2	Assistant property manager	3 years
3	Manager	5 years
4	Area property manager	10+ years

Job Responsibilities

Entry Level

THE BASICS: Answering phones. Keeping tenant files. Billing accounts.

MORE CHALLENGING DUTIES: Inspecting building upkeep. Arranging for repairs. Keeping in close contact with the building superintendent. Attending meetings with tenants. Working with community officials—police, sanitation, and other departments.

Moving Up

As you gain more experience, you might become involved in making reports on buildings in order to have them certified or recertified for government subsidies. You will begin to take on responsibilities from the office management—dealing with contractors or subcontractors hired to do particular repairs. The ability to handle a number of projects simultaneously and to satisfy the demands of many different people will stand you in good stead in your quest for more responsible positions.

ADDITIONAL INFORMATION

Salaries

SALES

Sales earnings are almost invariably in the form of commissions. Generally speaking, the firm gets 6 percent of the sale price, paid when a residential deal is closed. Of this, the broker gets half. In commercial work, the terms of a sales agreement vary, depending on how many principals are involved, whether the agent is handling the property management, the intended use of the building (i.e., development, upgrade and resale, or commercial leasing), and other considerations. Consequently, the commercial broker must be skilled at predicting and weighing the many factors that affect a sale.

When you begin, you can expect an annual income in the high teens or low twenties after your initial startup period. Commercial sales will bring you quickly into a high-income bracket. Many experienced commercial brokers make more than $100,000 a year and few make less than $50,000. Residential sales will yield a more moderate income unless your properties are very expensive.

APPRAISAL

In commercial appraisal, you'll start out in the low to mid- twenties annually, but after several successful years you will probably earn $30,000 to $40,000 per year. Senior appraisers can make $100,000 and more a year, if they're ambitious and their firms transact deals of significant size. Salaries are lower for those who go into residential appraisal.

PROPERTY MANAGEMENT

Entry-level salaries start in the mid-teens, but with several years' experience, your yearly salary can be in the $30,000 to $40,000 range.

Working Conditions

SALES

Hours: Your schedule will vary greatly from day to day because properties are shown during clients' free time. That often means you're on the job after five o'clock and on weekends. Many offices rotate floor duty among sales staff, who sign up for or are assigned shifts during regular office hours at least once, and sometimes several times, a week.

Environment: In commercial real estate you'll probably find yourself in comfortable office surroundings, with computers beeping, phones ringing, and typewriters clacking. To start, you will probably share an office with one or more people on the sales staff.

In residential sales, offices are attractive and are often located in a converted house, frequently one representative of the kinds of properties that the firm deals in. Condominium brokers frequently use one of their units as an on-site sales office until all the rest are filled. Firms also set up offices in shopping centers and business areas.

Workstyle: Count on a lively pace and lots of variety, at least in the periods when business is brisk. You might be out canvassing new sites or showing old ones. You might be on the phone answering queries or taking property profiles. At night, you could be closing a sale over dinner or taking classes.

Travel: You can expect to travel a lot in your immediate locality, but not much farther. Firms that take part in, or run, national referral services generally depend on the service to take care of business generated in distant places. Usually only the firm's officers and the more experienced company members attend realtors' conventions in other cities.

APPRAISAL

Hours: In the beginning, you will not be working much more than 40 hours a week. As you take on more responsibility and see projects through, you'll be coming in early, staying late, and working weekends.

Environment: Most appraisal offices are located in business districts in metropolitan areas. Offices will be comfortable and, without a doubt, computerized. To start, you'll share office space with others at the same general level.

Workstyle: Your time will be more or less equally divided among doing evaluations at property sites, researching records in government offices, and preparing reports and analyses in your own office.

Travel: Somewhat more opportunity for travel exists here than in sales. Contracts are often made with developers, builders, and investors in other parts of the country, where a large amount of on-site time will be required. An appraiser's jobs may include travel overseas, but rarely at entry level.

PROPERTY MANAGEMENT

Hours: Hours are usually nine to five, unless you must stay late to inspect a repair job or attend a tenant meeting.

Environment: Offices are hectic, since many people are involved in management, all with varying concerns and responsibilities.

Workstyle: You may spend as much time out of the office as in it during your first year, checking boilers for heat efficiency, monitoring tenant association meetings, or persuading local politicians to increase police protection at a shopping center. This in addition to your share of office duties.

Travel: There's virtually no travel, since the property you manage will be in the vicinity of your office.

Extracurricular Activities/Work Experience

College yearbook, newspaper, other campus publications—selling ad space

Campus fund-raising events—serving as a student adviser or helping with placement, working as a caretaker or superintendent.

Campus dormitories—working as a resident adviser

Internships

Because there are virtually no formal internships in the real estate industry, the best way to obtain experience is to contact a local real estate firm and apply for work during their busy season.

Recommended Reading

BOOKS

Appraisal of Real Estate (8th edition), American Institute of Real Estate Appraisers: 1983

The Art and Skill of Real Estate Selling: Fifty-eight Years in the Business by Reed E. Davis, Vantage: 1981

Modern Real Estate Practice: An Introduction to a Career in Real Estate Brokerage by Harry G. Atkinson and Percy E. Wagner, Dow-Jones-Irwin: 1984

Real Estate Management Trainee by Jack Rudman, National Learning Corporation: 1979

Real Estate Sales Handbook, Realtors National Marketing Institute: 1979

Real Estate Terms and Definitions by Andrew J. Maclean, Contemporary Books: 1982

Surviving and Succeeding in Real Estate by H.L. Poston, Prentice-Hall: 1982

PERIODICALS

Journal of Real Estate Education (quarterly), National Association of Realtors, 430 North Michigan Avenue, Chicago, IL 60611

National Real Estate Investor (monthly), 6255 Barfield Road, N.E., Atlanta, GA 30328

Real Estate Forum (monthly), 12 West 37th Street, New York, NY 10018

Real Estate Weekly (weekly), 235 Park Avenue South, New York, NY 10003

Professional Associations

The largest professional association is the National Association of Realtors(NAR), headquartered in Washington, DC, and Chicago, IL. It has eight major branches of operations:

American Chapter of International Real Estate Federation
American Institute of Real Estate Appraisers
American Society of Real Estate Councilors
Institute of Real Estate Management
Real Estate Securities & Syndication Institute
Realtors National Marketing Institute
Society of Industrial Realtors
Women's Council of Realtors

All have chapters or branch offices around the country. Most offer classes that are open to the public for fees ranging from $200 to $600. These are intensive daytime classes lasting from one to two weeks. Many local institutes are affiliated with the NAR, which exerts a strong influence on the field. Send queries to either of their two headquarters:

National Association of Realtors
430 North Michigan Avenue
Chicago, IL 60611

National Association of Realtors
777 Fourteenth Street, N.W.
Washington, DC 20005

INTERVIEWS

Richard Marchitelli, Age 36
Partner
Marchitelli & King Associates

I graduated in 1969 with a B.A. in political science from Belmont Abbey College, Belmont, North Carolina. I had always planned to attend law school. During college vacations, I worked in a real estate appraisal office doing research. I began to write portions of reports and was permitted to perform simple analytical tasks, and my interest in real estate appraising and consulting began to grow. Nevertheless, upon graduation from college I entered law school.

The more I became interested in appraising, the more I became disenchanted with law, so I left after one semester and worked full time for the appraisal company where I was employed during my vacations.

In 1973 I became one of two partners in the company where I was working. By 1975 my partner, who was much older than I, was preparing to retire. I felt that I was at a crossroads in my career and that in order to develop and grow professionally, perhaps I should join a national company. After much soul-searching and a series of interviews, I decided to stay in business for myself and took complete control of the company on the retirement of my partner.

At about this time, I decided to seriously pursue the M.A.I. designation, which I was awarded after fulfilling the demanding requirements. The M.A.I. designation has been invaluable on a business and a professional level. It gives me credibility in the marketplace. It indicates to our clients and other readers of my reports that I have achieved a level of competence that only 3 percent of practicing real estate appraisers have.

On the personal level, I have become very involved in the American Institute of Real Estate Appraisers, working on various local (i.e., chapter) and national committees. I meet regularly with real estate consultants from all over the country, exchanging ideas and viewpoints.

Currently I am serving the AIREA as vice chairman of the national publications committee, which is responsible for publication of all Institute textbooks. In this capacity, I also served as chairman of a special subcommittee that compiled and edited *The Dictionary of Real Estate Appraisal*. I was recently appointed to be 1985 chairman of the publications committee.

In 1982 Edward A. King, Jr. became a partner and principal in this company. The company formally changed its name to Marchitelli King & Associates, Inc. the following year. Currently we employ more than 17 persons.

The business itself is a demanding one. An appraiser must keep abreast of new theories and teachings by reading various professional journals and by regularly attending seminars and courses. Most important are the clients' demands, which center on service and competency.

Real estate consulting is also a pressure business. The inability to meet a deadline could result in the loss of millions or tens of millions of dollars to a client. Often many people are waiting for delivery of one of our reports, which could be used to assist in a lending decision, determine the economic feasibility of a project, aid in the disposition of sale of a property, advise on conversion to an alternate use, and other matters.

Much of my time is spent developing new business, keeping in contact with existing clients, and running the company. An increasing amount of my time is spent as a corporate manager and less as an appraiser. In fact, there are few assignments that I complete totally on my own anymore. My time is also spent reviewing a staff member's work. However, 99 percent of the commercial reports leaving the office are still personally reviewed by both my partner and myself.

Managing the business as a business has presented an additional challenge. My partner and I meet monthly to review the company's performance, monitor where recent business has come from, plan development of new business, and discuss where there might be a "window" in the market for our services, offering further diversified services. We also meet weekly with our office manager to discuss performance of the office.

At these meeting we review computer printouts of a program specifically designed to show how much business the company did the previous week, new business that came in, performance of individual staff members, in terms of workload, billings, and other areas.

My partner and I still complete special assignments in conjuction with one another or in combination with one or more staff members. Some recent such assignments include the valuation of the leased fee estate underlying the Stanhope Hotel on Fifth Avenue and 81st Street in Manhattan, appraisal of a 2200-acre tract of land with more than ten miles of coastline, preparation of a comparative tax study of industrial properties, a cost benefit study involving a luxury condominium project in New Orleans, and analysis of a joint venture opportunity for a bank consisting of a multiuse building (i.e., residential cooperative apartments, retail condominiums, and office condominiums).

My days are full and busy. They begin at 7 A.M. at the office and often end after 11 P.M. I often work on Saturdays and, once in a while, on Sundays. In addition to the constant pressure, they are filled with luncheon and dinner meetings, staff meetings, corporate business, and telephone calls.

I have been a contributor to professional journals in the past and have recently had an article approved for publication in the October 1984 issue of *The Appraisal Journal*, published by the AIREA. I am also planning to write article on the real rate of return, valuing cooperative apartment buildings, and deflationary economic pressures on real estate values.

I find the field of real estate appraising/consulting to be challenging and intellectually satisfying. Every day is different. There are always problems requiring new solutions. I could not imagine myself feeling as fulfilled as I do practicing law or doing anything else. I do not merely enjoy this business, I love it.

Real estate appraising can also be financially rewarding. A person with intermediate experience can earn from $35,000 to $50,000 a year. Senior people earn in excess of $100,000 annually.

James Giordano, Age 23
Salesperson
Rockland Realty
Spring Valley, NY

My family has had an insurance/residential real estate business since 1929. My uncle, the present owner, asked me to work for him while I finished my education. After a year and a half, I came to the realization that I didn't enjoy selling residential real estate. You literally work seven days a week and often show a property at seven or eight at night. The work is also very emotional. You must be totally involved and aggressive in making sales.

Since I am not the hard-sell type of person and I liked the industry, I knew I had to find something less emotional, less pressured, which led me to commercial real estate. You do not have to be as aggressive in finding commercial clients. Except in big cities, few realtors specialize in commercial real estate. If you understand the needs of commercial clients, you have a tremendous amount of potential business. At the time I left my uncle's business—about two years ago—I knew my present employer. He has an excellent reputation in the area. I walked into his office and said, "I want to work for you." He made me responsible for our commercial sales (most of our business is residential), although my title doesn't reflect that distinction.

I do a lot of what is known as franchise site selection. I find sites for well-known chains, such as fast-food restaurants. In those businesses, location is everything. You have to understand what type of site a company is looking for and, within a certain location, you must find a site that fits its needs. A marketing background can help you understand what a business is trying to achieve when it chooses a location.

Commercial sales is a 24-hour-a-day job in that you are always looking for real estate. Clients love for us to bring a piece of property to their attention—it saves them time. What you must learn—and you develop this only through experience—is how to spot a site and to recognize which business would be interested in it. The instant you see a vacant property on the highway, your mind has to start clicking—you see what else is nearby, what the general area is like, and you start mentally placing an operation on that site. If you enjoy this challenge, the job is not hard at all.

I am paid entirely on commission. In residential sales, if you make a sale, you might not get paid for three months; in commercial sales, you might not get paid for eight months! The ability to manage money is important—because when you get a commission check, you might not see another for two months. If you plan to go into real estate, you should have some savings.

The kind of people you find going into real estate are ones who are willing to take chances. When you start right out of college, you may not make much money, but the potential for big dollars is there. It is all a matter of being willing to take risks.

BIBLIOGRAPHY

The College Graduate's Career Guide by Robert Ginn, Jr., Charles Scribner's Sons: 1981

College Placement Annual by the College Placement Council: revised annually (available in most campus placement offices)

The Complete Job-Search Handbook: All the Skills You Need to Get Any Job and Have a Good Time Doing It by Howard Figler, Holt, Rinehart & Winston: 1981

Consider Your Options: Business Opportunities for Liberal Arts Graduates by Christine A. Gould, Association of American Colleges: 1983 (free)

Go Hire Yourself an Employer by Richard K. Irish, Doubleday & Company: 1977

The Hidden Job Market for the 80's by Tom Jackson and Davidyne Mayleas, Times Books: 1981

Jobs for English Majors and Other Smart People by John L. Munschauer, Peterson's Guides: 1982

Job Hunting with Employment Agencies by Eve Gowdey, Barron's Educational Series: 1978

Making It Big in the City by Peggy J. Schmidt, Coward-McCann: 1983

Making It on Your First Job by Peggy J. Schmidt, Avon Books: 1981

National Directory of Addresses and Telephone Numbers, Concord Reference Books: revised annually

The National Job-Finding Guide by Heinz Uhrich and J. Robert Connor, Doubleday & Company: 1981

The Perfect Résumé by Tom Jackson, Doubleday & Company: 1981

Put Your Degree to Work: A Career Planning and Job Hunting Guide for the New Professional by Marcia R. Fox, W.W. Norton: 1979

The Student Entrepreneur's Guide by Brett M. Kingston, Ten Speed Press: 1980

What Color Is Your Parachute? A Practical Manual for Job Hunters and Career Changers by Richard N. Bolles, Ten Speed Press: 1983

Where Are the Jobs? by John D. Erdlen and Donald H. Sweet, Harcourt Brace Jovanovich: 1982

INDEX

Account executive, 12, 112
Account services (advertising), 1, 2, 6, 7, 9, 10, 11–13, 14, 15
Administration: human services, 52, 57, 58–59, 62
Administration on Aging, 54
Advertising, 1–20
Advertising agencies, 3, 4, 12, 108
Advocacy: human services, 52, 59–60
Adweek, 14
Affirmative action, 89, 91
American Advertising Federation, 15
American Field Service, 43
American Friends Service Committee, 55
American Institute of Real Estate Appraisers, 129
American Marketing Association, 78, 79
Appraisal: real estate, 121, 124, 126, 129–31, 133
Art: education, 44

Banks, 124
Boys' Clubs of America, 54
Brand managers, 78
Breaking into the field, 4, 25, 41, 55, 75, 88, 109, 125
Brokers, 122, 128, 133
Business Research Practicum, 79
Buying: retailing, 22, 23, 27, 29

Cable television, 2, 23, 73
Career advancement: advertising, 6, 9, 11, 13; department store retailing, 24, 27, 29; human services, 50, 59; market research, 77; personnel, 91, 93; public relations, 112; real estate, 131, 132
Career paths: 6, 8, 10, 12, 43, 77, 90, 92, 95, 112, 128, 130, 132
Carter, Jimmy, 37
Certification, 41, 43, 45, 56
Chain stores, 27, 31
Chemical Marketing Research Association, 75
Church-affiliated institutions, 40, 55
Commercial real estate, 122, 125, 126–27
Communications department. *See* Public relations
Community mental health facilities, 54, 57
Community relations, 52, 61–62
Compensation and benefits (personnel), 86, 91–93, 96
Competition for jobs. *See* Job outlook
Computers, 7, 22, 38, 44, 61, 86, 87, 105, 172; in education, 38
Copy editor, 109
Copywriter, 2, 3, 5, 6, 109
Counseling (human services), 52, 56
Creative department (advertising), 1, 4, 5, 7, 10, 14, 15
Crisis intervention (human services), 56

Department store retailing, 21–36
Discount department stores, 28

Editing, 105
Education, 37–49
Employee/labor relations (personnel), 86, 94–96
Employee relations (public relations), 104
Employers, 3–4, 23, 24, 40, 54, 74, 87, 106–107, 108, 124–125
Employment: personnel, 86, 89–91
Employment agencies, 88, 89
Entry-level positions: advertising, 2, 9, 15; department store retailing, 22, 25, 29; human services, 52, 55, 58, 61, 62, 63; market research, 73, 75, 77; personnel, 86, 87, 88, 89, 90, 94, 95; public relations, 106, 108, 112, 113; real estate, 126, 128, 130, 132

Equal Employment Opportunity (EEO), 89, 91
Executive placement personnel, 88
Experience, prerequisite, 6, 8, 10, 12, 26, 28, 43, 77, 90, 92–93, 95, 112, 128, 130, 132
Experience, prior, 15, 21, 31, 45, 64, 79, 97, 114, 135
Extracurricular activities, 15, 31, 45, 64, 79, 97, 114, 135

Federal government, 54, 55
Federal Job Information Centers, 55

Geographic job index, 3, 23, 40, 53, 74, 87, 106, 123
Geriatric care, 53
Goodwill Industries of America, 54
Government agencies, 88
Grocery stores, 23
Guidance (human services), 56

Health care administration, 58
Health care facilities, 52, 58
House organs, 104
Human resources. *See* Personnel
Human Resources Information Systems (HRIS), 87
Human services, 51–69

International job opportunities, 25, 42, 55, 75, 89, 105, 126
Internships, 12, 16, 31, 45, 64, 79, 97, 115, 136

Job openings. *See* Job outlook
Job opportunities, new. *See* Job outlook
Job outlook, 3, 22, 39, 53, 73, 87, 105, 123
Job responsibilities: advertising, 6, 8, 11, 13; department store retailing, 26, 29; human services, 57, 59, 61, 62; market research, 77; personnel, 85, 91, 93, 95; public relations, 112; real estate, 128, 130, 132

Kissinger, Henry, 37

Labor laws, 94
Labor relations, 94
Local government: human services, 54

McIntyre, Pat: *Study and Teaching Opportunities Abroad,* 43
Management positions, 11, 13, 23, 27, 96. *See also* Store management
Market research, 13, 71–84
Media: advertising, 1, 2, 6, 7, 10, 11, 14, 15
Media placement, 105, 111
Member Appraisal Institute (M.A.I.), 129
Mental health facilities, 57, 63
Mentally retarded, 56, 57
Merchandising, 21, 22, 25, 27, 30
Merrill Lynch, 123

National Council of Accreditation of Teacher Education, 41
National Education Association, 43
National Institute of Education, 60
Nonprofit organizations, 52, 54, 108

Occupational therapy, 51
Office for Handicapped Individuals, 54
Office of Child Development, 54
Office of Naval Research, 61

Paraprofessionals, 54, 58; psychology, 52, 57
Parole officers, 60
Peace Corps, 43, 55
Personnel, 85–102
Placement office, college, 4, 21, 41
Placement organizations (education), national, 41–42
Planned Parenthood, 54
Plato, 37
Point-of-sale computer terminals, 22
Portfolio(s), 4, 5
PR. *See* Public relations
Probation officer, 60, 63
Professional associations, 17, 32, 47, 66, 80, 98, 116, 137–38

Program development: human services, 52, 62
Property management, 121, 131, 133
Psychologist(s), 54, 57
Public relations, 103–120
Public Relations Society of America (PRSA), 115
Public schools, 40, 43
Public speaking, 105, 111

Qualifications: advertising, 5, 8, 10, 12; department store retailing, 21, 26, 28; education, 43; human services, 51, 56, 58–59, 60, 61, 62; market research, 76; personnel, 90, 92, 94; public relations, 104, 111; real estate, 128, 130, 131

Real estate, 121–142
Recommended reading, 16, 32, 46, 65–66, 80, 97, 115, 136
Recruitment, 25, 75, 89; personnel, 86, 89–91
Relocation management, 127
Research: advertising, 1, 2, 7, 9, 10, 14, 15; human services, 52, 60; public relations, 105, 109
Research analysis, 9, 75–78
Residential real estate, 122, 125, 126–27
Retailing. *See* Department store retailing

Salaries, 14, 29, 63, 78, 96, 113, 133
Sales: real estate, 121, 126–29, 133
Sales license, 125, 131
Schirra, Wally, 38
Senior real property appraiser (S.R.P.A.), 130
Social service agencies, 52, 62
Social worker, 57
Special education, 39
Specialty stores, 23
State government: human services, 54
Store management, 22, 25, 30
Study and Teaching Opportunities Abroad (McIntyre), 43
Substance abuse programs, 53

Teaching. *See* Education
Technology, 2, 106
Teleconferencing, 105
Television, 3, 4, 7
Tolstoy, Leo, 37
Training, in-house, 51, 60, 86; department store retailing, 22, 25, 28, 29
Travel opportunities: advertising, 15; department store retailing, 31; education, 45; human services, 64; market research, 79; personnel, 93, 97; public relations, 114; real estate, 134, 135

UNESCO, 43
Unions, 94, 108, 111
U.S. Department of Education, 39
U.S. Department of Health and Human Services, 54, 60
U.S. Department of Justice, 54
U.S. Information Agency, 42

Variety store chains, 24
Veterans' Administration, 54
Video retailing, 23
Videotex, 2, 3
Viewtron, 3
Vinci, Leonardo da, 37
VisiCalc, 7
Volunteer work, 45, 55, 64

Wholesalers, 27
Word processors, 105
Working conditions: advertising, 14; department store retailing, 30; education, 44; human services, 63–64; market research, 78; public relations, 113; real estate, 134–35
Writing (public relations), 105

YMCA, 54

NOTES

NOTES

NOTES

NOTES

NOTES

NOTES

NOTES

NOTES

NOTES

NOTES

NOTES

NOTES

NOTES

NOTES